HOW TO REMOVE NEGATIVITY FROM YOUR LIFE

Develop the Power of Positive Thinking

RACHEL STONE

Copyright © 2021 by Rachel Stone

All rights reserved.

No part of this book may be reproduced in any form or by any electronic or mechanical means, including information storage and retrieval systems, without written permission from the author, except for the use of brief quotations in a book review.

Claim Your Freebie NOW!

Get Good At Problem Solving

Want to know the secret behind getting good at problem solving? Everyone seems to be able to do it, but you're stuck in the pile of endless to-do lists with little progress.

Ok, so how do I get my FREE book?

EASY! See the next page

Claim Your Freebie NOW

Instructions:

1. Open the camera or the QR reader application on your smartphone.
2. Point your camera at the QR code to scan the QR code.
3. A notification will pop-up on screen.
4. Click on the notification to open the website link

Grab your Freebie NOW

Instructions:

1. Open the camera or the QR reader application on your mobile phone.
2. Point your camera at the QR code to scan the QR code.
3. A pop-up menu will you up to scan it.
4. Click on the notification to open the website or link.

SCAN ME

Also By Rachel Stone

Start Being Fearless, Stop Being Scared

Fed up of being scared of the things in life that hold you back? It's time to take control back and start being fearless.

Also By Rachel Stone

Why Living a Simple Life is Better for You

An easy guide to help you change the way you think about your life. Take steps to start living a stress-free life.

Also By Rachel Stone

How To Heal Toxic Thoughts

Are you sick of your whole day being ruined due to your overthinking? Have you had enough of self-sabotaging everything good in your life? Do you want practical strategies to finally have a peaceful night's sleep?

Grab the Rachel Stone series NOW

Instructions:

1. Open the camera or the QR reader application on your smartphone.
2. Point your camera at the QR code to scan the QR code.
3. A notification will pop-up on screen.
4. Click on the notification to open the website link

Contents

Introduction	xvii
1. Why Do We Have Negative Thoughts?	1
2. How To Remove Negativity In My Own Head	5
3. Patterns Of Negative Thinking	7
4. Causes Of Negative Thinking	9
5. Cognitive Behavioural Therapy (CBT)	14
6. Why Do We Consider Things In The Way We Do?	27
7. The ABC Model	31
8. How to Spot Negative Thinking	33
9. The 'Shoulds' Tyranny	37
10. Awfulising	40
11. Discovering Negative Thinking	45
12. Disputing Negative Thinking	54
13. How To Remove Negativity In Relationships	65
14. Can Good Relationships Make You Happy?	67
15. Getting Unstuck From The Past	76
16. Mindfulness With Your Partner	81
17. Being Happy	91
18. Happy People's Attributes	94
Afterword	103
Feedback	105
Claim Your Freebie NOW!	107
Claim Your Freebie NOW	109
Also By Rachel Stone	111
Also By Rachel Stone	113
Also By Rachel Stone	115
Grab the Rachel Stone series NOW	117

Introduction

Have you ever spent hours or days ruminating over a matter only to discover that it wasn't that significant after all? Maybe you've had a situation when you were upset about something and then talked it over with a friend. They stated something you hadn't considered, and when you implemented their suggestions, you felt considerably better? Speaking with your friend provided you with a new perspective on your circumstance, and as you began to think differently, your feelings began to shift.

Every day, we encounter instances that exemplify the simple premise that our thoughts impact our feelings. Things go wrong, people act egotistically, and disappointments occur. Whether or not we are affected by them and how much anguish we feel is primarily determined by our thoughts. Even when our living circumstances aren't all that bad, we can make ourselves miserable by thinking in a negative, self-defeating manner. While we may blame others or life events for our misery, our perceptions cause us to suffer.

This is good news because, while we may not change people or our situations, we can alter our perceptions of them. We may stop disturbing ourselves unnecessarily if we learn to think in a healthy balanced way.

Our thoughts determine our outcomes.

From time to time, we all have negative thinking. However, if these thoughts frequently overpower you, you should investigate what you're thinking and how your thoughts affect your mental health. This internal monologue is an unavoidable aspect of your mental environment. It's always there, at all hours of the day and night, reminding you of the groceries you need to get, shaming you for missing your sister's birthday or making you nervous about current events (like politics, the environment, or the current state of the economy).

Even if you are not constantly aware of their persistent existence, these thoughts are the background noise of your life. Take a moment to pay attention to your thoughts right now. Stop them if you can. Isn't it difficult? You'll notice how they keep coming in, one after the other, uninvited and frequently undesired.

Some of your thoughts are illogical and useless. "My arm itches." "It appears that it will rain." "How did I lose my keys?"

Many of our ideas, on the other hand, are intrusive and negative. "He's a jerk". "I completely botched that project." "I'm really sorry for what I said to Mom."

These negative, neutral, or positive thoughts clutter our minds, just as they might clutter your home when you have too much stuff.

Unfortunately, getting rid of mental clutter isn't as easy as getting rid of an item. You can't just "throw" a thought away and expect it to go away. Your negative ideas, like a never-ending game of Whack-a-Mole, have a way of reappearing as soon as you slap them down.

1

Why Do We Have Negative Thoughts?

IMAGINE YOUR MIND as a well-organised home, devoid of the distracting, depleting, and unnecessary stuff that upsets you. What if you could only be surrounded by thoughts that uplift, inspire, and calm you? Consider your mind as a clear blue sky with no clouds, and you have the authority to pick what floats across it. Why do we think so much with so few filters to sort the positive and necessary thoughts from the random and unnecessary? If that cloudless mental sky is so desirable, why do we think with so few filters to sort the positive and necessary thoughts from the random and unnecessary?

Your brain has roughly 100 billion neurones, and your spinal cord has another billion. The total number of synapses between neurones—the cells that process information—is believed to reach 100 trillion. Our strong brains are continually processing and interpreting various events in the form of thoughts. What we consider to be reality is formed by our thoughts.

We can direct and control our thoughts, but it frequently feels as if they have their own minds directing us and how we feel. Thinking is vital for solving issues, evaluating, making decisions, and planning. Still, the mind roams like a wild monkey in between periods of proactive mental endeavours, pulling you through the brambles of rumination and pessimism. Your persistent inner dialogue keeps you from paying attention to what is going on in the present moment. It makes you miss out on important events and sabotages your joy of the present moment.

Surprisingly, we believe we need to "figure out" why we aren't as happy or fulfilled as we wish we could be by thinking more or harder. We attempt to find the things, people, and experiences to satisfy our desires and make us happy. The more we think about our sadness, the more depressed we get. Our thoughts make us feel restless, empty, and irritated as we project into the future or search the past for answers.

Almost every negative thought you have is about the past or the future. Even when you're anxious to escape the never-ending tape playing in your head, it's common to find yourself locked in a continuous cycle of regretful or anxious thoughts. You are struggling not only with your thoughts but also with your incapacity to be rid of them. The more negative thoughts you have, the worse you will feel. It's almost as if you're two people: the thinker and the judge, the person thinking the thoughts and the person aware of them and judging how horrible they are.

We become infected with painful emotions as a result of this thinking/judging process. We feel more pressured, nervous, depressed, and angry the more afraid, guilt-ridden, regretful thoughts we experience. Our thoughts can sometimes paralyse us with negative emotions, and it is these emotions that rob us of inner peace and serenity. Even though our ideas are the source of so much suffering, we assume there isn't much we can do about it. Isn't it true that you can't stop your mind from thinking? You can't turn your brain off at will, and you can't get rid of the mental clutter and feelings that keep you from completely enjoying life.

We occasionally experience unexpected mental serenity and silence. Most of the time, though, we try to quiet our minds by overindulging in food, alcohol, drugs, work, sex, or exercise. However, these are only transient acoustic and pain relief measures. Our minds are soon drawn back to it, and the cycle repeats. Is it inevitable that we will always be victims of our "monkey minds"? Do we have to fight our thoughts all the time, allowing them to weigh us down with worry, regret, and anxiety? Is it possible to have a mind that is free of negativity and pain? You may not be able to keep your mental house clean all of the time, but you may influence your ideas in such a manner that it improves your quality of life and general pleasure. While thinking may appear to be uncontrollable and automatic, many of our thought processes are automatic and, well, thoughtless.

Although you and your ideas may be inextricably linked, you do have a "conscious self" that may intervene and govern your thoughts. Your ideas are significantly more under your control than you may believe. When you learn to regulate your thoughts, you open the door to a world of creativity, inspiration, and brilliance that lies just beneath the clutter. You can disempower your thoughts and create more "room" in your mind to enjoy inner peace and happiness through various mindfulness practices and practical habits. You'll be able to prioritise what matters most in your life, what no longer supports your goals, and how you want to live daily.

This book is meant to provide ideas and examples that demonstrate how simple it is to achieve happiness. In short, if you implement the ideas in this book, you will have a happy and fulfilled life. We have arrived at a point in history when our civilisation has become the playground's biggest bully. Numerous stressful scenarios can strike an individual left, right, and centre. It's heartbreaking to see people succumb to the concerns, responsibilities, and challenges of human existence. We must learn to change our thinking and stay positive in any situation because we can't change how our environment bombards us with things to worry about.

People who think positively about a circumstance are more likely to succeed in life than those who think negatively about a scenario. Nowadays, being optimistic is not only a choice but a must. It's how you'll get by in the jungle with only a few scratches.

This book will teach you how to see the bright side of any situation. You'll learn how your ideas, whether positive or negative, may have a huge impact on your life and how to start eliminating the negative ones. You will realise how critical it is to develop a positive thought habit and put it into practice in your daily life. We encourage you to take the first step toward becoming the positive person you've always wanted to be. Begin turning the pages of this book, and you'll be well on your way to a more prosperous and happy existence. It all starts with you.

2

How To Remove Negativity In My Own Head

SURELY, you have at some point in your life come across various websites advising you to stop thinking negatively to feel better about yourself? This approach is as effective as removing the odour of a particular food to prevent the smell from spreading throughout the house without removing the food! Even if you get rid of the odour, it will reappear in the food. Unless you get rid of the food, the odour will remain there.

The smell of irrational beliefs is a negative thought. If you tell yourself that people will laugh at you every time you try to give a presentation, this does not indicate that you should restrict your negative thinking; rather, it means that you should analyse your beliefs to understand why you are thinking that way.

One of the most common causes of such ideas is a perception that you are incompetent or useless in general. Negative thoughts do not emerge from your mind unless there is a source that generates them. This is the source of false beliefs.

Another type of negative thinking, which is based on what we learned as children, leads to false beliefs. As children, we were exposed to uninformed parents, relatives, teachers, and friends who may have passed on to us some unfavourable thinking patterns that can help us establish negative thoughts.

In the next section, we'll look at those patterns and show you how to break them so you can stop misleading thoughts from forming.

3

Patterns Of Negative Thinking

LACK OF CONFIDENCE stems from mistaken views about oneself and incorrect evidence is one of the key contributors to establishing these false beliefs. It's critical to understand how most individuals mistakenly interpret information and how their thinking habits might be the germ that leads to negative views at this point.

The following are some of the most well-known negative thought patterns that contribute to the establishment of negative beliefs.

- **ALL-OR-NOTHING THINKING:** If I don't do everything correctly, I'll be considered a failure. The most hazardous aspect of all-or-nothing thinking is that it might cause a person to doubt their abilities and capabilities after a single disappointing performance. If you find yourself thinking in this manner, tell yourself that you are thinking negatively and that one situation does not define your worth. Remind yourself of the past occasions in which you performed admirably so that you can recognise and dismiss this style of thinking as soon as it emerges.

· · ·

- **IGNORING POSITIVE EVENTS:** Neglecting positive events, such as attributing a compliment to a person's kindness rather than your own worthiness, is one of the most dangerous thought patterns. The reason you think you're no good and haven't been complimented before is that you threw away all positive remarks as soon as you got them, and your subconscious mind buried them deep!

- **LABELLING:** We've already addressed the process of labelling, but it's worth noting that labels don't just influence you during a circumstance; they stay with you as long as you continue to support them with false facts, and so never allow you to feel confident.

- **CATASTROPHISING** entails constantly assuming the worst-case situation. For example, during the presentation, I will forget everything, everyone will laugh at me, and I would be considered extremely boring.

- **MIND READING:** One of the most well-known negative thinking patterns, which inhibits a person from feeling confident by supplying him with a plethora of misleading evidence to back up his false ideas. "She didn't say hello because she thinks I'm boring," for example, is a well-known example of mind reading.

- **OVER-GENERALISATION:** When a huge group of people acts like one of them, this is known as over-generalisation. Over generalisations, such as believing that attractive women are arrogant, are particularly widespread. While some attractive women can be arrogant, who said that all attractive women are arrogant?

4

Causes Of Negative Thinking

BEFORE WE GET into the numerous exercises for overcoming negative thinking, it's crucial to understand why you develop these thoughts in the first place. So, in this section, we'll look at four reasons why people think negatively.

EVERYDAY STRESS

Many people feel overwhelmed by life because they are under a lot of stress. The stress caused by information overload, physical clutter, and the never-ending decisions needed can lead to various mental health concerns such as generalised anxiety, panic attacks, and depression.

Sleep issues, muscle discomfort, headaches, chest pain, repeated infections, and stomach and intestinal illnesses may result if you combine this stress with reasonable worries and concerns in your life, according to the American Psychological Association (not to mention dozens of studies supporting the connection between stress and physical problems).

THE PARADOX Of Choice

When it comes to mental health, the freedom of choice, which is prized in free societies, can have a declining point of return. The expression "paradox of choice," coined by psychologist Barry Schwartz, sums up his findings that more choice leads to more anxiety, hesitation, paralysis, and discontent. More options may provide objectively better outcomes, but they will not make you happy.

Consider a simple supermarket shopping trip. According to the Food Marketing Institute, the average store held 42,214 goods in 2014. What used to be a 10-minute trip to the store to get the essentials now takes at least that long to decide on the best yoghurt brand or the best gluten-free crackers. If you want to buy a pair of jeans, a wardrobe classic, you'll be greeted with a never-ending list of options. Is this a baggy fit? What about a bootcut? Skinny? Do you have a wide leg? What about a vintage wash? Is it a button fly? Zipper? It only takes a simple purchase to have you hyperventilate.

Steve Jobs, Mark Zuckerberg, and even President Barack Obama have chosen to limit their clothing options to avoid getting overwhelmed when making decisions. The president described his limited outfit choices in an essay with Vanity Fair written by Michael Lewis:

Obama stated, "You'll see I only wear grey or blue suits. I'm attempting to make fewer choices. I don't want to have to make decisions about what I'm going to eat or wear. Because I have a lot of other things to think about."

Too Much "Stuff"

Our homes are cluttered with clothes we never wear, books we never read, toys we never play with, and technology we never use. Our computer inboxes are bursting at the seams. Our desktops are disorganised, and our phones are displaying notifications such as "You require more storage."

We've become such gadget slaves that we'd rather have the instant gratification of instant information or entertainment than real-world connections and experiences. Thanks to the constant flow of information and access to technology, it's easier than ever to become mass consumers of things and data. We can order anything from a book to a motorboat and have it supplied to our house with the press of a button.

We're stuffing our houses with stuff we don't need and filling our days with tweets, updates, articles, blog entries, and cat videos. We are surrounded by information and material, but we feel powerless to do something about it.

All of this useless information and data waste our time and productivity and cause us to think in reactive, nervous, and negative ways.

Like:

"My Facebook buddy appears to be content with her life. My life is a shambles."

"Should I get the FitBit and start tracking my health to make sure I don't die too soon?"

"Oh great, I completely forgot about that 'How to Make a Million Before You're 30' webinar—what if they revealed anything crucial?"

EVERYTHING APPEARS to be crucial and urgent. Every email and text message must be responded to. It is necessary to get the most up-to-date device or gizmo. This keeps us continually agitated, preoccupied with small matters, and disconnected from the people around us and our own feelings.

We frequently believe that we don't have time to declutter because we're too preoccupied with consuming new information. But, at some time, all of this activity will exhaust us mentally and emotionally. We analyse, ruminate, and worry ourselves to death as we process everything that comes our way.

How did we lose sight of the principles and objectives that were used to keep us grounded and sane? What are our options? We won't be able to live in a world without technology if we go back in time. We can't give up all of our material possessions and live in a cave. We must find a method to existing in this modern environment while maintaining our sanity. Decluttering our belongings and limiting our time spent on digital gadgets might help reduce anxiety and negative thinking. However, there are still plenty of reasons for us to get caught in the mental clutter of negative thinking, stress, and regret.

We are concerned about our health, jobs, children, economy, relationships, how we look, what others think of us, terrorism, politics, past trauma, and our uncertain futures. Our thoughts about these things cause us pain and detract from the joy we could be experiencing right now if we didn't have that continual voice in our heads stirring things up.

THE NEGATIVITY BIAS

The human nervous system has been developing for 600 million years, yet it still reacts the same way it did when our forefathers faced life-threatening conditions daily and had just to survive.

Any negative thought that penetrates your mind feels real, so you incline to believe it. However, you are not living in a cave and are not faced with life-threatening events daily. You don't have to accept your inclination to think negatively just because you were born that way. There's a better way than merely connecting with the next notion that comes to mind. Mindfulness is an alternative. Mindfulness can be cultivated by particular exercises presented throughout this book, and it can be practised in even the most routine occupations.

Mindfulness entails retraining your brain to focus on the current moment rather than the mental clutter of the future. You don't cling to your thoughts while you're conscious. You are simply present in whatever activity you are engaged in.

Sounds simple, right?

Although the premise is deceptively simple, altering your mindset is not so straightforward.

Like any other habit, decluttering your mind takes effort, patience, and a willingness to start small and progress from there. Fortunately, we'll show you how to do everything in this book.

You'll not only learn how to train your brain and regulate your thoughts, but you'll also develop the habits that will help you maintain these mental practices regularly.

We'll go through several behaviours you can employ to clear

your mind in the next section. You'll notice that as you control your thinking, you'll become more focused and productive, as well as more at ease with all of life's chaotic demands.

So let's get started with the first habit that will help you rewire your brain.

5

Cognitive Behavioural Therapy (CBT)

COGNITIVE BEHAVIOURAL THERAPY (CBT) is a psychotherapy technique used by therapists to assist people in achieving positive change by addressing their cognitive patterns, moods, and behavioural concerns. CBT is used to identify and treat problems with irrational thinking, dysfunctional beliefs, and improper learning. Individuals, organisations, and families can all benefit from CBT, which aims to restructure one's beliefs, perceptions, and responses to support behavioural changes.

Sigmund Freud's mind and approach to psychological therapy dominated Western psychiatry throughout the first half of the twentieth century. Freud thought that all psychological disorders stem from repressed unconscious longings from childhood, and his therapy approach, known as 'psychoanalysis,' entailed daily sessions, often lasting years, to explore the depths of his patients' unconscious minds. The goal of psychoanalytic therapy was for patients to gain insight into the source of their misery and, as a result, be free of suppressed urges and the psychological anguish that accompanied them. Other psychotherapy treatments began to emerge in the 1950s. Some were directly developed from Freud's theories (such as "psychodynamic," "existential" and "humanistic" psychotherapies), while others adopted a completely different approach. The most important of these became known as Cognitive Behavioural Therapy (CBT) later on.

Albert Ellis, a psychologist, and Aaron Beck, a psychiatrist, were two of the most prominent figures in CBT development. Both began their careers as Freudian therapists, only to become disillusioned with psychoanalysis in the end. Albert Ellis criticised Freud's basic theories as well as the excruciatingly gradual study of early experiences that were central to psychoanalysis. Ellis began to focus on the function of thoughts and beliefs in causing psychological suffering in the early 1960s. He claimed that people upset themselves by thinking unreasonably and that psychological issues may be handled by educating them to think rationally and with balance. He devised a treatment that urged patients to pay attention to what was going on in their lives and question some of the irrational thoughts and underlying beliefs causing them pain. The name of Ellis's therapeutic approach was modified from 'Rational Therapy' to 'Rational Emotive Therapy (RET) to reflect the goal of therapy, which was to use rational reasoning to improve emotional responses. The name was modified to Rational Emotive Behaviour Therapy (REBT) in the 1990s to reflect the importance of behavioural methods in this approach.

Aaron Beck was a pioneer in the creation of cognitive-behavioural therapy (CBT) for depression. He discovered that depressed people had defective or distorted thought patterns. These are the result of schemas, which are foundational ideas formed in childhood in reaction to early life events and influence how we view our experiences later on. Beck defined schemas as "templates" that we employ unconsciously to determine the meanings we assign to our experiences. Schemas such as 'I am inferior,' 'people can't be trusted,' 'I will be abandoned,' or 'the world is hazardous' influence the content of individuals' thinking in everyday settings, contributing to unhappiness and psychological issues. Beck, like Ellis, believed that the goal of therapy should be to assist patients in recognising and changing flawed thinking and self-defeating behaviours through a variety of cognitive and behavioural methods.

While Ellis coined the term "irrational" to describe ideas and beliefs that cause emotional pain, others have used adjectives such as "negative," "maladaptive," "unhelpful," "unrealistic," "faulty," and "self-defeating." Throughout this book, different names are used interchangeably to communicate the idea of thoughts, beliefs, and perceptions that cause us to feel terrible or act in self-defeating ways. While different schools of CBT utilise different techniques and terminology, the overall goal is to help people relieve suffering by changing unhelpful cognitions and behaviours. Since Ellis and Beck initially described their theories, CBT treatments for specific issues have been improved and updated several times. More effective treatments continue to emerge as research uncovers fresh facts.

CBT Strategies

The following are examples of CBT strategies:

COGNITIVE STRATEGIES INCLUDE LEARNING to recognise the negative thinking habits that cause distress and employing various techniques to develop more rational ways of thinking.

BEHAVIOURAL STRATEGIES INVOLVE ENGAGING in a variety of behaviours that assist us in changing the way we think and feel. These include behavioural studies, repeated exposure to fearful circumstances, deep relaxation and breathing methods, problem-solving, goal planning, assertive communication, social support, and activity schedule.

IN RECENT YEARS, several CBT therapies have included the third component:

MINDFULNESS STRATEGIES INCLUDE PAYING full attention to present-moment events with an open and curious mindset. This includes being aware of one's breath, thoughts, emotions, or physical sensations as they emerge. Thoughts become objects of the mind rather than 'reality or 'truth' due to meditation and careful attention during regular life events.

Cognitions

OUR COGNITIONS ARE mental processes that include the ideas, beliefs, and attitudes we use daily. Some of our cognitions are conscious, while others may be brought to our consciousness with little thought. Other cognitions are unconscious and may need more precise processing to bring to consciousness. Others, on the other hand, will always be unaware.

Our ideas and beliefs are not the same things, despite their similarities. Thoughts are fleeting and frequently aware. It is believed that the average human has between 4,000 and 7,000 thoughts every day. We are typically unaware that we are thinking; but, if we pause and study our present ideas. Our ideas have an impact on how we feel and behave.

Beliefs are relatively constant and typically unconscious assumptions about ourselves, others, and the world that we hold. Although we can actively think about our ideas and even question their truth at times, we don't do so most of the time. Our beliefs impact the content of our thoughts, as well as our emotions and behaviours.

Emotions

WE'VE ALL EXPERIENCED what it's like to be pleased, sad, scared, furious, disgusted, or astonished, but what precisely are emotions? They are, in fact, difficult to define. Emotions, in general, can be defined as the way we feel in our minds and bodies in reaction to events that occur. They are caused by a trigger, which might be:

- an **external** occurrence (for example, noise from next door; a friend's statement) or
- an **internal** occurrence such as a bodily sensation (e.g., pressure in the chest, a surge of heat) or a cognition (e.g.,

'I said something stupid,' 'I'll be alone all day,' 'I did a fantastic job').

The resultant emotions are a mix of cognitive assessments and physiological responses. The meaning we assign to an experience determines our cognitive evaluation (how we think about things). So, if your buddy does not answer your call, you may be furious ('She only calls when she wants something'), anxious ('I hope she's OK'), indifferent ('She's so busy; I'll have to call her again'), or wounded ('She doesn't care about me'). Our evaluations can be easily brought to awareness; nevertheless, it might be difficult to recognise what we perceive at the moment (for example, when you are unhappy, afraid, or angered but don't know why).

Physiological reaction (e.g., increased heart rate; tightness in tummy muscles or chest; feelings of heat, arousal, heaviness, etc.) — Because emotions usually entail physical experiences, people are often advised to 'notice what's going on in your body to connect with their emotions.

Emotions Influence Behaviour

Emotions developed as cues to encourage behaviour and aid in survival. They focus our attention on issues we believe to be relevant and drive us to respond by doing something by making us feel good (e.g., pleasure, love, excitement) or unpleasant (e.g., worry, guilt, hurt, despair). If we want to feel good feelings while avoiding unpleasant ones, both emotions play a part in motivation. However, the desire to avoid unpleasant emotions is the larger motivator.

Unpleasant feelings draw our attention to situations that require our attention and drive us to take action. This allows us to do tasks that benefit our well-being.

As an example:

- Kirstin's anxiousness pushes her to finish her essay over the weekend.
- Neil's anger drives him to talk assertively with his boss.
- Corrine's loneliness propels her to join a singles club.

- Sid's remorse drives him to switch off the television and take his kids to the park.

HOWEVER, we might sometimes respond to unpleasant feelings by numbing them rather than addressing the situation they warn us about. Our actions may give temporary comfort, but they do not address the underlying issue, and as a result, the negative emotions continue to haunt us.

As an example:

- Cheryl avoids paying her taxes because she finds them tedious.
- Laura avoids medical visits due to health concerns.
- Leonie uses poker machines to dull her anger and fear.
- Chris avoids social situations because they make him feel depressed and inept.
- Jim drinks excessively in response to his emotions of remorse.

PLEASANT FEELINGS ARE OFTEN USED as a "carrot" to persuade us to make compromises in the "now and now." Working long hours, going to the gym, cleaning the house, or putting in a long day with the kids are all typically undertaken with the idea that the rewards (feeling good) will arrive later. Long-term benefits that encourage us to put our current goals on wait are pleasant emotions such as joy, personal fulfilment, feelings of security, or self-worth. However, as with unpleasant feelings, pursuing them might lead us to engage in self-defeating behaviours. This can happen when we choose short-term pleasures above long-term advantages, such as living over our means, partying too much, or chasing an exciting romance that we know will end in sorrow.

. . .

COGNITIONS AFFECT emotions

Our cognitive evaluations, or how we think about what is going on in our lives, determine our emotions. Some examples are shown below:

Cognition = Something awful may occur.
Emotion = Anxiety.

Cognition = They did something wrong, and they shouldn't be allowed to get away with it.
Emotion = Anger.

Cognition = I did something wrong, and I deserve to be punished.
Emotion = Guilt.

Cognition = Everything is going swimmingly for me.
Emotion = Contentment.

Cognition = I've lost something important to me.
Emotion = Sadness.

Cognition = The world is a horrible place, I am a useless individual, and the future looks uncertain.
Emotion = Depression.

Cognition = I did something immoral, and others believe I'm a horrible person.
Emotion = Shame.

Cognition = Things aren't going as well as they should.
Emotion = Frustration.

Cognition = Something excellent is on the way.
Emotion = Excitement.

Cognition = That is abhorrent.

Emotion = Disgust.

Cognition = Others are superior to me.
Emotion = Inadequacy.

Cognition = I am a terrible person.
Emotion = Self-Loathing.

Cognition = That was not what I was expecting.
Emotion = Surprise.

Cognition = She/he does things on purpose to harm me.
Emotion = Contempt.

Emotions have an impact on cognition

Our cognitions not only impact our emotions, but our emotions also influence our cognitions. Indeed, the emotions we are experiencing affect the 'content' of our thoughts and the interpretations we assign to current events. For example, many of our thoughts revolve around a perceived injustice and a desire for vengeance when we are upset. When we are sad, we perceive situations negatively, frequently experiencing failure, hopelessness, and rejection when none exist. When we are nervous, we focus on risks and begin to see danger in circumstances that we would ordinarily dismiss as harmless.

Behaviours

Behaviours encompass how we react in certain situations as well as our daily habits and routines. Our cognitions have a significant impact on our behaviour. Here are a few examples:

Cognition = Everyone has to like and approve of me.

Behaviours = Excessively attempt to satisfy people; avoid forceful behaviour.

Cognition = I have to do everything right.
Behaviours = Procrastinate; work slowly and ineffectively.

Cognition = Making errors is an opportunity to learn, not a disaster.
Behaviours = Willing to try again — and again, if required — to achieve goals.

Cognition = People should follow my lead and do what I feel is right.
Behaviours = Unfriendly or angry toward people who fail to live up to expectations.

Cognition = I am likeable and valuable. People respond well to me.
Behaviours = Willingness to reach out to others, form connections, and take social risks.

Cognition = My life should be simple; I should avoid doing activities that are difficult or unpleasant.
Behaviours = Avoid tasks that are difficult or unpleasant, even if they are beneficial.

Cognition = I'm a failure.
Behaviours = Try not to learn new stuff.

Cognition = I need someone stronger than myself on whom I can trust; I can't do it independently.
Behaviours = Continue to be in dysfunctional, loveless, or toxic relationships; accept abusive treatment.

Cognition = I can do anything I set my mind to if I am prepared to put in the effort.

Behaviours = Willing to put in the time and effort to achieve goals.

Cognition = If I want anything, I must have it right away.
Behaviours = Engage in addictive behaviour, such as consuming alcohol, smoking, using drugs, eating a poor diet, and so on.

Cognition = Everyone is giving it their all. No one is worthy of being judged or condemned.
Behaviours = You get along well with the majority of individuals.

Cognition = I have faults; I am not okay.
Behaviours = Avoiding eye contact and taking social risks while self-monitoring in social interactions.

BEHAVIOUR'S INFLUENCE Emotions and Cognitions

While our emotions impact our behaviours, the opposite is also true: our behaviours influence our feelings. This occurs in two ways. Initially, certain behaviours have a direct mood-boosting effect. Second, some behaviours influence our cognition, which in turn influence how we feel.

BEHAVIOUR'S DIRECT Mood-Enhancing Effect

We've all been in circumstances when adjusting our behaviour made a difference in how we felt. Perhaps, when you were feeling low, you decided to call a buddy, which helped you feel better. Perhaps you engaged in some physical activity, music or were immersed in an intriguing project. These activities can raise our spirits since they are naturally enjoyable and divert us from negative thoughts. It is also uplifting to do tasks that offer us a sense of accomplishment or purpose. As a result, clearing out a cabinet, painting a room, writing a letter, or completing a difficult task might make us feel wonderful.

Behaviour's Indirect Effect on our Feelings — via Cognitions

Many of our actions help to reinforce pre-existing beliefs. Avoiding social interaction, for example, might promote the notion that we are not OK or that people dislike us. This might result in feelings of loneliness, sadness, or low self-esteem. Unassertive behaviour for the majority of the time may perpetuate the notion that it is not appropriate to ask for what we want. The behaviour reinforces our emotions of inadequacy. Choosing to avoid situations that we are afraid of confirms our notion that those circumstances are really dangerous. As a result, whenever we have to encounter certain situations, we get apprehensive. Attempting to accomplish everything flawlessly all of the time promotes the notion that everything we do must be perfect. As a result, we feel nervous or immobilised in circumstances where we may not perform flawlessly.

Changing some of our behaviours, on the other hand, might help us think differently about our circumstances and feel better as a consequence. For example, starting social interaction may assist in challenging the idea that we are incapable of making friends, and our new cognition — 'I can make friends when I put in the effort' — may make us feel better about ourselves. Confronting our fears — the feared social event, the speech, or that nasty phone call — can cause us to cease viewing such situations as extremely dangerous, and our updated cognitions — 'I can manage it; it's not that awful' — assist to lessen our anxiety in those situations. Completing certain activities less than flawlessly can assist us in realising that things do not have to be perfect, and this updated belief relieves us of unneeded tension. Communicating assertively to settle a disagreement might help us realise that we are capable of overcoming some difficulties and, consequently, feel happy. Doing some activities that we keep putting off (for example, filing your tax return, inviting the in-laws for dinner, or painting the bedroom) might help us see that they aren't that awful after all, reducing our guilt and irritation and increasing our confidence. And, believe it or not, being polite to someone we detest may help us see them more favourably and make us feel more at ease in their company. Through their effect on our cognition, all of these behaviours can make us feel better.

Cognitions, emotions, and behaviours all interact and affect one another. Understanding interdependence is beneficial because it reminds us that making a positive adjustment in one of these areas will positively impact others.

CBT is more than simply "positive thinking."

If you read popular psychology and self-help books, you've definitely come across books that claim positive thinking can be attained by constantly repeating specific affirming words. Typical examples include:

- I am rich and successful.
- I'm growing better and better every day in every aspect.
- My world is brimming with bounty.
- Everything is working out in my best interests.
- I approve of myself and love myself.
- The universe looks after me with love.

Many individuals use statements like these to try to think more optimistically, but do they work? The answer is: it depends on whether you believe them or not. Affirmations might serve to reinforce the information that we already know but disregard. For example, reminding ourselves of our talents, accomplishments, and the people who love us might help us maintain a positive attitude at times. Reciting statements we don't believe, on the other hand, will not magically imprint them on our unconscious mind. The emphasis in CBT is on realistic, balanced thinking rather than wishful thinking.

APPROPRIATE VERSUS INAPPROPRIATE Emotions

The goal of CBT is not to eradicate all negative feelings but to respond properly to situations. There are times when it is reasonable and proper to be sad, remorseful, furious, or dissatisfied. It is natural to be sad when we lose something we care about. It is natural to be dissatisfied when we fail to meet a certain goal. If we do something that we later find has caused harm to another else, it is natural to experience remorse. It's natural to get irritated when someone else does something we think is unfair. Psychologically healthy responses produce emotions that are appropriate for the circumstances. As a result, we feel regret rather than debilitating guilt, disappointment rather than devastation, concern rather than overpowering anxiety, sadness rather than depression, and annoyance rather than anger.

As we've seen, negative emotions may be beneficial when they inspire us to take action to better our condition. Unpleasant feelings, for example, may push us to apologise, communicate, arrive early, complain to the boss, focus on a job, make apologies for hurting someone, or seek a second opinion.

Grief, for example, is an appropriate emotion at times. Most individuals will experience sadness when a loved one dies, their house is lost, they are diagnosed with a terrible disease, or they lose a long-held desire. The agony of a big loss can continue for years, and while time eventually cures or at least lowers the grief, the scar is typically left behind. Unfortunately, there is no quick route out of sadness. Even in mourning, though, negative thinking can cause more unneeded pain.

6

Why Do We Consider Things In The Way We Do?

BECAUSE COGNITIONS PLAY such a significant part in how we feel and behave, the question arises, 'Why do I think this way?' And why do some individuals think in a healthy, balanced way the most of the time, while others have negative, prejudiced, and self-defeating beliefs the majority of the time? The solution can be found in the many influences that have influenced our thinking throughout our lives. The most significant are:

Early infancy — the ties created with our parents throughout our infancy as a result of their affection, availability, and responsiveness to our needs.

Childhood experiences — the messages we got from our parents and important individuals (e.g., grandparents, siblings, teachers, schoolmates, etc.) during childhood and adolescence.

Temperament — inherent elements of our personality (i.e., biologically determined).

Early events in our lives have an impact on how we think and feel later in life. Individuals who were lucky enough to grow up with loving, emotionally attentive, and rational parents are more likely to develop the ability to cope with stress or hardship than those who were not. Those who endured childhood neglect, trauma, or abuse, on the other hand, are more prone to develop emotional issues later in life. While early life experiences are essential, even people with wonderful parenting might develop psychiatric issues since temperament impacts how we think and feel. Individuals who experienced misfortune as children, on the other hand, can acquire a good psychological view in maturity owing to their intrinsically resilient character.

Other variables impact our thinking at various periods of life, in addition to our early life experiences. These are some examples:

· important connections in our life, such as those with our spouses, friends, family members, and coworkers;

· important events, including victories, defeats, triumphs, and rejections;

· the messages we receive from popular culture through social media, television, billboards, magazines, newspapers, and movies; and

· the knowledge and information we gain from different sources, such as the internet, reading, courses, and educational institutions.

The Influence Of Temperament

While there is no gene for distorted thoughts, biological factors impact how we respond to circumstances and give them significance. Our temperament is a biological component of our personality.

Temperament characteristics are frequently apparent in early life, perhaps as early as a few months of age. Some people are born with a neurological system that is extremely sensitive to change or threats, making them more vulnerable to distressing emotions such as anxiety, sadness, and anger. Some people have a very nervous temperament, and as a result, they interpret many neutral occurrences as dangerous ('Why is that vehicle going down this street?'; 'Why is my right cheek so red?'). Others have a melancholy temperament and are thus more inclined to see themselves and their experiences negatively ('I have accomplished very little today'; 'I have failed again again'). Some people are introverted by nature, and as a result, they may be particularly shy or sensitive in social circumstances. They may interpret rejection or disapproval in reaction to neutral social settings ('Why did they sit over there, rather than next to me?'; 'He just glanced away – he is bored with me'; 'She laughs when she speaks to my colleagues, but not when she speaks to me). And some people have a fractious temperament, which causes them to overreact or become irritated in situations that do not affect others.

Although biology might affect our psychological inclination, unpleasant sentiments are not inescapable. People who have a biological predisposition to cardiovascular illness do not always experience a heart attack or stroke. They must, however, work more than others to maintain a nutritious diet, obtain regular exercise, and lower cholesterol levels. Similarly, people with a temperament that makes them more likely to experience distressing emotions must work harder to manage their cognitions and behaviours than those with a robust temperament. CBT techniques can assist us in developing more cognitive flexibility and, as a result, resilience. This will minimise the frequency and severity of distressing feelings, allowing us to recover more quickly in circumstances where we do become upset.

Societal messages

Many of the messages we get from popular culture contribute to our dissatisfaction by affecting our views. Social media, television, movies, billboards, and publications all emphasise the value of things like:

- having a lot of money and material goods.
- Popularity entails having a large number of friends.
- Career success is defined as having a high-status, well-paying employment.
- Being youthful and appealing.
- Having pleasant, harmonious family connections.

People believe these messages to varying degrees. Many people feel that they must have a high-paying job and costly consumer goods, be slim and young in appearance or have many friends to be successful. The more deeply we hold our views, the more likely we are to be dissatisfied when our real circumstances do not match them. For example, if you believe that you must have pleasant, harmonious family connections, but your family relationships are dysfunctional, believing that things must not be this way makes you unhappy or inadequate. While there is nothing wrong with desiring to have pleasant family connections, attractiveness, friends, accomplishments, or financial prosperity, believing that things must be a specific way is a sure way to generate unhappiness.

7

The ABC Model

MOST OF US believe that the things that happen to us cause us to feel the way we do. For example, when we are angry, worried, irritated, or sad, we are prone to blaming others or our situations. However, as Ellis pointed out, events and people do not make us feel good or terrible; they only serve as stimuli. It is our cognitions that influence how we feel.

Ellis created the **ABC model** to demonstrate this:

- The letter **A** stands for 'activating event,' which is the condition that causes us to react.
- **B** stands for 'beliefs,' or our perceptions of the circumstance.
- The letter **C** stands for 'consequences,' which include emotions (including bodily sensations) and behaviours.

While we often blame 'A' (the triggering event) for 'C' (the repercussions), it is 'B' (our beliefs) that causes us to feel the way we do. Consider the following simple example:

- Assume you are running late for an appointment and are feeling stressed.

- Running late for an appointment is an activating occurrence.
- Physical strain, worry, fretting, and unsafe driving is all effects of C.

You are nervous and apprehensive, and you are driving dangerously (C), not because you are late (A), but because of your beliefs (B) about punctuality and the repercussions of being late. Some of your beliefs may include, 'I must always be punctual; 'People will not like me if I am late'; 'People should approve of me'; and 'The repercussions are likely to be terrible.'

D: Dispute Introduction

Ellis introduced the term "dispute" to represent the process of questioning our preconceptions about events. Once we've identified the thoughts and beliefs that make us unhappy, the next step is to dispute them. For example, in the above scenario, we may tell ourselves, 'My prior experiences have taught me that even when I'm running late, I typically arrive on time or a little late.' I prefer to be on time, and I generally am, but it is unlikely to have serious effects if I am late on this occasion.

CBT relies heavily on the debate. Learning to modify rigid, inflexible cognition allows us to avoid or let go of feelings that bring unneeded discomfort. In the above scenario, we could feel worried rather than overly anxious. It may also drive us to change our behaviour, such as not driving dangerously.

8

How to Spot Negative Thinking

WHAT DO you think the world's happiest individuals would have in common if we gathered them all together? A lot of money? What about their looks? Professional success? Others' awe and admiration? Wrong! Those with the most adaptable mindsets are the happiest. Are any of the individuals you consider to be truly happy (most of us can count them on the one hand) rigid, demanding, or uncompromising? Do they become agitated when things do not go their way?

The capacity to adjust to changing circumstances — a skill known as cognitive flexibility — is a fundamental attribute of happy individuals. This does not imply that they are weak or indifferent; in fact, they are frequently eager to work on important issues. They are, nevertheless, ready to recognise that certain things are out of their hands. Many of the problems we face in our daily lives are the result of rigid, inflexible thinking.

Illusory Beliefs

Albert Ellis noted that most individuals are predisposed to think in illogical and self-defeating ways by nature. He observed that certain people are susceptible to unpleasant emotions because they think in self-defeating ways. Our thinking is illogical, according to Ellis, if it contradicts our basic need for happiness and long life. So, if holding a specific belief causes you to suffer inappropriate anger, irritation, worry, despair, or feelings of worthlessness, or if it interferes with your capacity to enjoy good health and long life, the belief is irrational, according to Ellis' definition. This includes attitudes that lead to self-defeating behaviours, including procrastination, social avoidance, violence, and ignoring our physical health. Ellis highlighted numerous illogical ideas that contribute to pain and psychological suffering, including frequent irrational beliefs.

Common Irrational Beliefs

CONSEQUENCES

Everyone has to like and approve of me.

= Anxiety, lack of assertiveness, sadness, and low self-esteem.

In every way, I must be competent, adequate, and successful.

= Anxiety, self-deprecation, sadness, frustration, humiliation, and procrastination.

The world should be a fair place, and I should be treated fairly at all times.

= Anger, resentment, frustration, and despair.

People should share my values and views and conduct themselves in the same manner as I would.

= Anger, bitterness, and strained relationships.

Certain people are terrible, and they should be held accountable or punished for their actions.

= Anger, resentment, hate, and sadness.

When I make a mistake, I am a horrible person, a failure, and an idiot.

= Frustration, sadness, and low self-esteem.

The world should give me what I require. Life should be enjoyable. I shouldn't have to suffer or be inconvenienced in any way.

= Dissatisfaction, sadness, and despair.

It's horrible when things don't go the way I want them to.

= Irritability, rage, and depression.

Living circumstances create human sadness, and it is hard for me to be happy when things aren't going well.

= Procrastination, unsolved issues, and relationship issues.

If there is a potential that anything awful may happen, I should think about it right now.

= Anxiety, persistent worry.

Every problem has the right answer, and it's terrible if I can't discover it.

= Uncertainty, procrastination, and anxiety.

. . .

WHILE THESE ARE JUST EXAMPLES of typical illogical ideas, hundreds more might be added to the list. We shall examine additional ideas that lead to uncomfortable feelings throughout this book.

9

The 'Shoulds' Tyranny

WHEN WE BELIEVE that things *should* or must be a certain way, we expose ourselves to discomfort rather than just having a choice. Ellis referred to this lack of flexibility as 'demandingness' since we have an inherent need for things to be a specific way. American psychiatrist Karen Horney coined the term "tyranny of the shoulds" in 1939 to characterise this concept. **'Shoulds'** are the guidelines or ideas we have about what is required in our society. Some of our 'shoulds' are about what we expect of ourselves, while others are about how people should behave and how the world should be. While not everyone has a strict thinking style, most people have at least some 'shoulds' that cause unpleasant emotions from time to time.

MANY OF THE FOLLOWING 'SHOULDS' lead to problems. Can you name some that had an impact on you?

- I should always execute a flawless job.
- I should never make mistakes.
- I should always be efficient with my time.
- My life should be simple and uncomplicated.

- I should be treated fairly at all times.
- I should always be able to exert control over the occurrences in my life.
- Other people should always do what is seen to be the "correct" thing.
- I should be liked and approved of by others.
- I should be thin, young, and appealing.
- In whatever I do, I should be knowledgeable and effective.
- I should be doing and doing more.
- I should always be completely self-sufficient.
- I should constantly be positive, pleasant, and optimistic.
- I should be married or in a serious relationship.
- I should have a happy, loving, and supporting family.
- I should be an excellent parent.
- I'm supposed to be seductive and have a strong libido.
- I should be at work.
- I should have a high-ranking position.
- I should be able to make a lot of money.
- I should be funny, fascinating, and enjoyable to be around.
- I should be like everyone else.
- I should have a lot of friends.
- I should be as intelligent as the smartest individuals I know.
- I should always say 'yes' to other people's demands.
- Never should I feel scared or insecure.

These ideas might make us feel unpleasant since our actual experiences do not always correspond to them. For example, the notion that "Everyone must like and approve of me" causes issues when we say or do anything that may evoke criticism from others. We may not be as young or thin as we would want to be, nor do we have a high-paying career or a great marriage. We may not be as intelligent, witty, or engaging as we would like to be. We make errors, others disapprove of us, our performance suffers, problems arise, and friends disappoint us. The more certain we are that it cannot be this way, the more distressed we get.

What makes us miserable is not so much the content as it is the rigidity of our ideas. When beliefs are regarded as desires, they are not an issue. We won't be unhappy if all we want is job success, excellent relationships, independence, or a comfortable existence, as long as we recognise that it doesn't have to be this way. It is also completely acceptable to desire others to do what we feel is right and treat us fairly, as long as we are flexible enough to realise that this will not always happen. Life always requires us to be adaptable. When things don't go as planned, we may either make ourselves miserable by insisting that it shouldn't be this way, or we can change and go on by choosing to think more flexibly.

A word of warning: some people place much too much importance on uttered words rather than their underlying meaning. Simply removing the words "should" and "must" from your vocabulary does not make you a free thinker. It is not the words we employ but the beliefs we have that are important. Being adaptable necessitates the modification of our cognitions, not simply our words.

10

Awfulising

ELLIS CREATED the word **awfulising** to explain our propensity to exaggerate the unpleasant parts of our lives. Awfulising (also known as 'catastrophic thinking' or 'catastrophising') is a condition in which we perceive unwanted or unpleasant events as more aversive than they need to be. Consequently, we cause distress that is disproportionate to our living circumstances, whether we are dealing with little inconveniences or major issues. When our thinking is maladaptive, seemingly little occurrences like being kept waiting, having to spend time with someone we don't like, appearing stupid in front of others, or forgetting an appointment might feel terrible. Even more significant issues, such as losing a job or being involved in a vehicle accident, will cause mild, moderate, or severe discomfort depending on our cognitive style.

'Shoulds' and 'awfulising' are inextricably linked, as both represent cognitive rigidity. We get irritated when things don't go our way because we believe the repercussions will be disastrous. As an example:

- I must do it thoroughly — it's horrible to make mistakes.
- People must like and appreciate me — it's awful to be disliked.

- I must find a companion — it's awful to be single.
- It's terrible to be overweight, so I should be slim.

We learn not to awfulise by gaining cognitive flexibility. This enables us to deal with the inevitable hiccups.

KEEP AN EYE ON YOUR THOUGHTS.

Our thoughts function as an inner voice, reflecting our impressions of what is going on in the world. Usually, we are not aware of our ideas; they simply run in the background of our minds. However, if we pay close attention, we can frequently recognise some of their components.

Many of our thoughts are emotionless: 'I should allow the cat in,' 'I need to return that phone call,' 'I need to remember to pick up that delivery,' 'Do these shoes match this top?' Some of our thoughts elicit more noticeable, positive emotions: 'I did a really good job'; 'Hallie took her first steps today;' 'This is going to be a lot of fun!'; 'That dog is lovely'; 'They're such kind people — I believe they loved me.' Other thoughts elicit negative, distressing emotions: 'What a fool I am! I really messed up'; 'I despise doing this! What a bore!'; 'They'll think I'm foolish'; 'He's late again;' 'How normal!' Negative or prejudiced thoughts often elicit unpleasant feelings. However, because much of our thinking occurs without our awareness, we rarely notice our ideas unless we take the time to observe them.

Tuning in to our ideas allows us to recognise those that are inflexible, irrational, or prejudiced. Recognising that our views are irrational might sometimes help us see things differently. At times, we need to push them more forcefully using a thought monitoring form. In either case, it is beneficial to keep track of our thoughts, especially when we are feeling down.

Patricia planned to go out with her girlfriend on Saturday night, but her girlfriend had to cancel at the last minute. It is now too late for Patricia to make alternate plans. Patricia is depressed. 'Everybody is going out and having a wonderful time, but I have nowhere to go,' she thinks to herself. 'It's really depressing.'

While it is understandable for Patricia to be frustrated by the last-minute cancellation, does she need to be depressed? Her cognitions will determine whether she feels indifferent, dissatisfied, angry, enraged, or heartbroken. Patricia is upset because she believes:

- On Saturday evenings, everyone goes out and has a fantastic time.
- I'll be missing out if I don't go.
- I should always go out on Saturday evenings. It's terrible to have to stay at home.

Patricia must become conscious of her cognitions and confront the rigidity of her thinking to change the way she feels. For example, she may convince herself, "I prefer to go out on weekends, and I generally do." Saturday night is a popular night out for many individuals, but it is not for everyone. Even if I did go on dinner with a buddy, I wasn't certain to have a great time. Now that I'm not going out, I can watch a movie and play computer games. Staying at home tonight is disappointing, but it is hardly the end of the world.'

Rachel had planned to travel overseas with her partner for a long time, but she became ill with glandular fever in the last two months and has been quite ill. She no longer has the energy or desire to go a week before her departure date. Rachel is worried and guilty because she does not want to let her lover down. 'This is a really awful thing for me to do — he will be extremely disappointed,' she thinks to herself.

While it is understandable for Rachel to be sad for not keeping her commitment, is it essential for her to feel guilty and anxious? Rachel has the following beliefs:

- Once I've made a decision, I should stick to it no matter what.
- I should constantly prioritise the needs of others. I should never do something that will cause people to be disappointed.
- I'm a horrible person because I let someone down.

Rachel will need to gain some cognitive flexibility to see her position more rationally. This will include questioning some of her 'shoulds' (for example, 'I like to be reliable, and I generally am, but occasionally it isn't feasible'). This is not to suggest that her boyfriend's sentiments are unimportant. Going out of our way for people we care about is a natural component of human interaction. However, occasionally things do not go as planned, and we cannot achieve our obligations despite our best efforts. Rachel will control her emotions more successfully and sustain good relationships if she communicates openly and honestly.

Dennis has recently finished his senior year of high school. He has worked hard this year and has set his sights on studying law at university. Dennis learns from his findings that his grades were insufficient to go into law school. Dennis is in a bad mood. 'I have worked so hard this year — all that sacrifice for nothing!' he thinks to himself. 'What a waste of a year! My future has been destroyed.'

It's understandable for Dennis to be unhappy at having missed out on something he really desired. It is natural for him to be unhappy for a while as he comes to terms with his disappointment and plans his future. However, Dennis's pessimism is affected by his beliefs, which include:

- I must always achieve the objectives I set for myself.
- My future is compromised if I do not study law.
- The ramifications of this situation are disastrous.
- Life should be equitable – if I work hard for something, I should always receive it.

Conscious and unconscious thoughts

Although we can typically recognise our thoughts by just watching them, this is not always the case. For example, when Janet turns on her computer to begin working on her essay, she may feel her anxiousness growing, but she is unaware that she has any thoughts. Similarly, when Tyler prepares to leave work on Friday afternoon, he notices a drop in his mood, though he isn't aware of any specific thoughts. And Julie is nervous when she visits a psychologist for the first time, even though she is not consciously thinking anything.

While our ideas are not always aware, we can generally recognise the feelings that they elicit (anxiety, sadness, guilt, embarrassment, worry, anger). These emotions reveal information about the substance of our thinking.

Try this practice if you're having trouble recognising your thoughts: Close your eyes and ask yourself, "What is going on in my life right now?" Spend two minutes observing your inner environment – your feelings, bodily sensations, pictures, and thoughts. Thoughts from the "back of the mind" (just below consciousness) will frequently become evident.

When Janet paused to consider what was going on in her head, she realised: 'So much work to accomplish and so little time!' Tyler realised his thoughts were on the same theme: 'The weekend has arrived, and there is nothing for me to look forward to,' while Julie was thinking, 'This psychologist may not be able to assist me, and I may never heal.'

Have you ever gone into a room full of strangers and felt a surge of anxiety? What are the thoughts (conscious or unconscious) that could be causing anxiety in such a situation?

11

Discovering Negative Thinking

AARON BECK OUTLINES several typical examples of incorrect thinking (reasoning mistakes) that contribute to emotional discomfort in his book Cognitive Therapy of Depression. These are more common in sad persons, although even when they are not depressed, most people make reasoning mistakes at times. Beck and other researchers recognised the following as some of the most prevalent examples of erroneous thinking.

THINKING in black and white

This is the inclination to perceive things in polarised terms, with little regard for the centre-ground. For example, you may label people or events as good or terrible, positive or negative, successes or failures. This thinking is illogical because of the inability to recognise that most circumstances fall somewhere in the middle.

People with perfectionist tendencies are more prone to black-and-white thinking. In the above example, when Dennis tells himself, "Not going into law means I've destroyed my future," he demonstrates black-and-white thinking. Dennis ignores the reality that he has numerous alternatives that may lead to favourable outcomes by believing that anything other than his initial desire is completely undesirable.

Henry had spent months working on a report, and after finally submitting it, he noticed a mistake in one of the parts. Even though the error has no serious implications, Henry is distraught. 'I really messed up that report,' he thinks despondently to himself. Henry's thinking is black-and-white because he believes that "until everything is flawless, it is a disaster." The inability to perceive the middle ground — generally a positive report — gives Henry extra anguish and stops him from recognising his accomplishment.

Overgeneralising

Overgeneralisation occurs when we form unfavourable judgments about ourselves, other people, and life events based on little data. Sometimes it just takes one experience for us to begin thinking in words like "always," "never," and "everyone." For example, 'Whenever things start to look better, something bad always occurs'; 'Every time I attempt to communicate, I get nowhere'; 'I always screw up'; 'I haven't accomplished anything important in the last ten years; 'I'm a failure at work and in my relationships.'

Olivia hasn't communicated with most of her married friends since her marriage ended two years ago. Her seclusion began after she learned that one of her girlfriends suspected Olivia of flirting with her spouse. After first being irritated, Olivia decided, 'Now that I am single, I am a threat to my female friends - they believe I'm going to take their spouses.' Olivia was driven to give up on numerous connections due to this overgeneralisation, which contributed to his loneliness.

Personalising

When we personalise, we feel responsible for situations that are not our fault, or we mistakenly believe that other people's reactions are intended for us.

Evelyn is irritated by a coworker who seldom says hi as he walks by her in the office. Evelyn hasn't considered that her coworker suffers from significant social anxiety and that his behaviour reflects his shyness rather than any negative emotions toward her.

When someone is unpleasant to us, it is much more difficult not to personalise.

Ethan was annoyed when his supervisor was harsh with him about a small issue. Although he originally took it personally, Ethan afterwards realised that his boss was under a great deal of stress and that his violent outburst mirrored his own vulnerable state. Consequently, Ethan remained loyal and supportive of his boss, which was subsequently acknowledged and appreciated.

It is simple to become angry and trade insults with or "write off" someone rude; it is more difficult to comprehend. Recognising that other people's behaviour reflects their personality and state of mind and choosing not to take offence takes awareness and cognitive flexibility. However, doing so has significant long-term advantages, including good relationships.

FILTERING

Many of our experiences are influenced by our negative ideas about ourselves, other people, and the world. For example, we may find ourselves focused solely on the bad aspects, dismissing any other pertinent information. Our minds are immediately attuned to occurrences that reinforce our preconceptions, anxieties, and fears, while we block out information that contradicts those beliefs. As a result, if you are anxious by nature, you will focus on evidence that the world is dangerous while disregarding information that contradicts this viewpoint. If you have low self-esteem, you will notice any occurrences that indicate you are inept or hated while dismissing evidence indicating you are competent and appreciated. And if you feel that the world is hostile and uncaring, you will notice information that validates your beliefs while filtering out evidence that people are nice.

Rita just had her first radio interview, and the producer afterwards informed her that it went well, especially for a first performance. Rita was disappointed rather than thrilled with the good responses. The statement, in her mind, focused on her inexperience and indicated that she was not good enough. Rita misinterpreted the statement as a criticism rather than a compliment since she focused solely on her "debut performance" while disregarding the other opinions.

HAVING a negative mindset

Many of us are prone to jumping to unfavourable judgments in various situations, despite the lack of evidence to back them. When things go wrong, we may assume the worst or take other people's words or motivations in the most unfavourable way.

Evelyn is conducting a survey of a huge number of single moms for her Honours thesis. She has written two letters outlining the nature of her research to a single mother's website, hoping that they will be ready to notify eligible volunteers about it. After receiving no response, Evelyn believes that they are clearly opposed to researchers and refuse to assist. She subsequently finds that the website is managed entirely by volunteers and is frequently abandoned for days or weeks at a time.

READING people's minds

This is a leap of faith based on the idea that we know what other people are thinking. We think that people will judge us negatively without any evidence that this is the case. When we mind-read, we not only feel bad, but we also act in self-defeating ways.

Len wants a partner but is terrified by his friend's suggestion that he try internet dating. 'What if someone I know stumbles upon my profile on the website?' They'll think I'm desperate!' he tells a friend. Furthermore, Len hates attending parties or social gatherings because he believes everyone is staring at him and passing judgment on him. As is typical in similar situations, hardly one recognises Len or pays him any attention. However, Len's belief that people are evaluating him causes him to engage in self-defeating behaviours, such as avoiding chances that could allow him to obtain what he wants.

BLAMING

Things happen wrong in our lives from time to time, people disappoint us, and unanticipated catastrophes occur. While some individuals are willing to accept setbacks and human flaws, others are driven to blaming and criticising others for their flaws. Blaming is typically excessively simple since it fails to recognise the various elements that contribute to outcomes and the individuals we hold accountable. It also spends our energy on feelings of rage, bitterness, and resentment, preventing recovery.

Harold is still blaming the firm where he worked for six years for his dismissal two years later. Despite the situation's complexities, Harold blames management for holding a grudge against him and failing to recognise his years of devoted work. While it is understandable for Harold to experience anger or sadness, his urge to continue blaming and ruminating is counterproductive. It does not affect Harold's circumstances, but it takes away his peace of mind. Harold begins to feel better only when he begins to accept the past events and makes plans for the future.

LABELLING

Everyone is capable of making mistakes. We all make mistakes or do stupid things from time to time, and there are certain things that we simply aren't good at. We occasionally behave improperly, make dumb comments, do things that negatively influence others, perform poorly at work, ignore indications of declining health, make poor financial decisions, or fail to accomplish our goals.

Our cognitive flexibility is reflected in how we think about our mistakes or perceived faults. Sometimes it's logical and acceptable to remind ourselves, "That was a stupid thing to do — I need to be more careful," or "I'm not particularly motivated to clean the home," or "My memory isn't as good as it used to be." These thoughts do not generate issues because, while they identify faults or perceived shortcomings, they are specific rather than universal.

When we describe ourselves as an idiot, a failure, unattractive, no good, dumb, lazy, a loser, or inept, we are making broad generalisations about ourselves based on specific behaviours or experiences.

As a result, our self-esteem suffers, and we experience distressing emotions such as humiliation, self-loathing, and feelings of inadequacy. Labelling is the ultimate overgeneralisation because it ignores that individuals are a complex combination of characteristics and behaviours that cannot be described by just one or a few of them.

While some people label themselves, others label others: 'that man is a jerk," my boss is a moron," my sister-in-law is a nasty,' or 'that politician is a sleaze-bag.' Labelling others is just as irrational as labelling ourselves because we sum up a whole person based on specific behaviours or qualities. Labelling others is also counterproductive since it creates anger, consumes our energy, and makes it more difficult to get along with others. This is not to say that we should never pass judgment on the behaviour of others. It is quite acceptable to believe that a person's behaviour was irrational, unfair, unethical, or foolish, just as it is to believe that our behaviour is unreasonable, unfair, unethical, or silly. However, it is critical to distinguish between the individual's behaviours and the person as a whole.

Martha worked for six months at a legal company with terrible work standards and an indifferent culture. Martha made mistakes in several of her cases due to insufficient training and a lack of access to counsel, and as a result, she received unfavourable feedback from her supervisor. Martha saw herself as incompetent and a failure when she ultimately quit the company. Labelling herself in this manner harmed her confidence, making it difficult for her to obtain another employment.

When things don't go as planned, it's always good to assess the issue and think critically about the reasons. Identifying the causes that contributed to our unpleasant experiences, rather than labelling ourselves as failures, allows us to learn from those events without hurting our self-esteem.

PREDICTING disaster

Some people tend to focus on the negative possibilities - failure, rejection, loss, suffering, or disaster. *What if?* is a common phrase used in self-talk concerning impending calamities. For example,

'What if I lose my job and can't pay my bills?'; 'What if I make a fool of myself in front of all those people?'; 'What if I become sick and can't do what I promised?'; 'What if I don't know anybody and have no one to speak to?' By focusing on the chance that something will go wrong, we create anxiety in the present and lose our capacity to engage with what is going on around us completely.

Megan works as an independent interior designer. Megan instantly thinks that when some of her clients are sluggish to pay their bills, they will default, and she begins to anticipate the worst-case scenario. Although almost all of her customers pay their bills in the end, Megan is quick to envision scenarios of dispute, litigation, and threats. This causes worry, which diverts Megan's attention away from her present work.

Kathryn grew concerned after informing one of her coworkers about her breast cancer diagnosis. Kathryn has urged her coworker not to tell anybody, but she is still concerned that others may find out. Kathryn wonders to herself as she lies awake at night, "What if she tells someone, and then everyone finds out, and then it gets back to management, and they decide I'm a terrible risk?" They'll think less of me... It might have an impact on how people see me...'

Trevor has muscular twitching from time to time, but he is afraid to go to the doctor because he believes it is a sign of a dangerous neurological condition.

The fact is that the world is fraught with danger. Megan, Kathryn, and Trevor are worried about things that may happen, but the chances are small. They generate worry and anxiety by overestimating the likelihood of negative events, depriving themselves of ease of being. The difficulty is to learn to live with uncertainty, especially in situations over which we have little control. This entails accepting that bad things can happen (though they seldom do) and accepting that even if they do, we will deal with them when the time comes.

COMPARING

Many people evaluate their position, achievement, and personal worth by comparing them to others. Comparisons may be confined to their own peer group members – friends, relatives, individuals their own age, or classmates. Alternatively, they may be produced with a larger group of people, including the affluent and famous – media stars, corporate moguls, and politicians. Comparing might make us feel inadequate since there are always others who perform better than us in any particular field.

Sara was thrilled as she suited up for the workplace Christmas party. However, upon her arrival, she felt depressed. She felt ugly when she realised how gorgeous some of the other women were. To make matters worse, one of her coworkers had dropped 10 pounds and looked amazing!

JUST WORLD FALLACY

A frequent human reaction is the idea that things should be fair. That would be true in a perfect world, but we don't live in an ideal world. Many things in life are not fair, and believing that they should cause us anger and bitterness. Logan has just been informed that he will need to relocate due to the upcoming reorganisation and that another staff member will be taking over his office. Logan is furious by this decision's unfairness. He's put in a lot of effort since he got this job, so why should he have to leave?

While it is understandable to be upset when something is unfair, harbouring anger for an extended period makes our life unpleasant. Sometimes we have to accept that life is unfair and focus on the things we can control.

Some things are under our control, while others are not.

We have to figure out which is which.

LOOKING backwards

When we reflect on the acts we have made in the past, we may see those that have resulted in bad repercussions. We may convince ourselves that we should have realised our decision was bad at the time and that if we had done things differently, we would be much happier now. This sort of 'hindsight vision' is frequently referred to as 'shoulda, woulda, coulda,' as we ponder on all the things we should or could have done differently in retrospect.

Because we are continuously functioning with inadequate information and awareness, hindsight vision is illogical. Our current level of knowledge constantly binds the decisions we make at any time. We don't know the outcomes of our acts in advance since we aren't fortune tellers. As a result, claiming that we should have done things differently makes no sense.

Second, we assume that an alternative option would have yielded a better result. But how do we know this? We will never know the implications of taking a different road since we did not take it. Because many acts have unintended repercussions, we can't say if other choices would have better results.

Sophia finds herself wondering what her life would have been like if she hadn't married Stephen. 'I had so many guys to select from; why did I choose him?' she often thinks. Although they have been married for 30 years, and it is now too late to divorce, Sophia can't help but wonder whether she could have had a better life.

12

Disputing Negative Thinking

It is beneficial to be aware of our ideas. The practice of seeing and labelling illogical thinking (e.g., 'I'm personalising again,' 'I'm mind-reading,' or 'I immediately jumped to another negative conclusion') might help us see things more clearly. Furthermore, learning to challenge negative cognitions and discover a more balanced perspective can aid in the development of a more healthy cognitive style. Let's now look at some particular disputing strategies.

Logical Disputing

Upsetting emotions are frequently generated by rigid, unrealistic, or illogical thinking. One strategy for dealing with this sort of thinking is to engage in rational debate. This entails questioning our thinking's rigidity (that is, our belief that things must be a certain way) and discovering a more balanced viewpoint. Here are some examples of logically contradictory assertions that might be used to dispute commonly held irrational beliefs.

Logical Disputing Statements

Everyone has to like and approve of me.

Alternatively: I prefer that people like me, but expecting everyone to like me is unrealistic. I can cope even if some people don't like me, just as others can if I don't like them.

IN EVERY WAY, I must be competent, adequate, and successful.

Alternatively: I am skilled in certain areas but not in others. While I can try to improve my abilities, there is no reason why I should be proficient in all areas.

THE WORLD SHOULD BE FAIR, and I should be treated fairly at all times.

Alternatively: I like fairness, but I recognise that the world is filled with unfairness. A lot of things aren't fair, and I'm sure I'll face some injustice at some point.

PEOPLE SHOULD SHARE my values and views and conduct themselves in the same manner as I would.

Alternatively: People have the right to hold values and beliefs that differ from mine, and they will occasionally say or do things that I can't entirely agree with. It would be wonderful if people always did what I consider to be right, but there is no reason why they should.

CERTAIN INDIVIDUALS ARE EVIL, and they should be held accountable for their acts.

Alternatively: People can be unfair or thoughtless at times. I can criticise bad behaviour, but I don't have to denounce or condemn them as individuals.

When I make a mistake, I am a horrible person, a failure, and an idiot.

Alternatively: I, like everyone else, make mistakes or do stupid things from time to time, but it does not make me a failure or a terrible person. I've done millions of things in my life, and labelling myself based on just a few of them is both ridiculous and self-defeating.

The world should give me what I require. Life should be enjoyable. I shouldn't have to suffer or be inconvenienced in any way.

Alternatively: It's wonderful when things go well for me, and they do a lot of the time. But there's no reason why things have to be perfect all of the time. Obstacles are an unavoidable aspect of life.

It's horrible when things don't go the way I want them to.

Alternatively: It's frustrating and inconvenient when things don't go as planned, but it's rarely horrible or disastrous.

It is simpler to avoid issues than it is to address and resolve them.

Alternatively: Avoiding my difficulties may make things easier in the short term, but not in the long run. It is frequently useful to venture outside of my comfort zone to address difficulties and fix them.

Life conditions are the root source of human misery. It's difficult for me to feel joyful when things aren't going smoothly.

Alternatively: Even when things aren't going well for me, I can still feel good. My life is made up of many various parts, and I can enjoy certain portions of it while experiencing major challenges in others.

IF THERE IS a potential that anything awful may happen, I should think about it right now.
   Alternatively: Dwelling on events over which I have no control produces worry rather than changing the result. Rather than speculating on what could or might not happen, I can choose to deal with issues as they emerge.

EVERY PROBLEM HAS A SOLUTION, and I should be able to figure it out.
   Alternatively: Most problems do not have one proper answer but several viable ones. Our judgments can only be based on the facts available to us at the moment, and there are frequently no clear options.

Remember To Write It Down

We will see many examples throughout this book of how negative or faulty thinking may be logically challenged. Some cognitions are simpler to dispute than others, and those less entrenched may frequently be intellectually questioned. Most concepts and beliefs, however, are more successfully questioned in writing. Identifying the cognitions that lead to discomfort, writing them down, and then writing words that question those cognitions can aid in the transformation of foggy thoughts into clear concepts.

Writing also provides:

- Another level of processing.
- Reinforcing fresh viewpoints.
- Rereading those sentences aids in the consolidation of knowledge.
- A written record of rational statements can also be used as a reference guide in the future.

De-catastrophise

The words 'awfulising' and 'catastrophising' reflect our inclination to overestimate the negative consequences of our circumstances. Exaggerating the badness means that we perceive our circumstance as actually catastrophic, even if it is usually simply unwanted or uncomfortable. If we think about it, every unfavourable event may be perceived as a disaster. Worrying about life events might cause us to feel extremely worried, irritated, guilty, humiliated, sad, or resentful.

This is not to imply that nothing may be disastrous or horrifying. Contracting an extremely painful, progressive, incurable disease, becoming the victim of a vicious attack, losing a loved one, or becoming seriously handicapped due to an accident are all very terrible occurrences.

However, the majority of the things that go wrong in our life aren't all that awful. Most individuals admit that the great majority of the things that irritate them fall somewhere between 0 and 20 on a scale of awfulness. Even while making a foolish statement to someone we admire, missing a trip, or losing a contract may feel like a huge tragedy at the moment, the consequences are typically not that awful in the grand scheme of things. The problem is that when we awfulise, we perceive events as though they are completely terrible — at around 100 on the awfulness scale.

AM I MISTAKEN?

Here are some easy questions to help you put things into context:

- Have I ever felt like this before? Have I ever been wrong?
- Will this be relevant in five years?
- How terrible is this on a scale of 0 to 100?
- [Think of someone you know who is always positive.] What would their reaction be to this situation?
- Is this anything I can change? What can I do to help?

- Is there anything positive to be said about this situation? What do I have to be thankful for?
- What can I take away from this experience?
- What could possibly go wrong? What's the worst that might happen? What is the most likely scenario?

SOCRATIC QUESTIONING

Some negative thoughts are quite simple to fight, and merely acknowledging that our thinking is unreasonable might help us feel better. In other cases, it is beneficial to doubt the veracity of our beliefs. Socratic questioning is named after the Greek philosopher Socrates, who asked provocative questions to challenge people's beliefs about the world. Socratic questioning aims to subject our ideas to logical scrutiny, discover any evidence that contradicts them, and arrive at a more reasonable conclusion.

Depending on the context, many different sorts of Socratic questions can be asked. The following are some generic questions that may be used in a variety of circumstances. These inquiries are frequently referred to as "reality-testing" since they entail looking at objective data rather than depending on gut impressions. These questions are especially helpful when we leap to negative conclusions or make irrational assumptions.

REALITY EVALUATION

1. What exactly are facts?
2. What are my own perceptions?
3. What proof backs up my beliefs?
4. Is there any proof that contradicts my perceptions?
5. Am I making any logical errors?
6. In what other way can I interpret this situation?

Rodney was involved in an unfortunate event at work during a morning tea celebration. Rodney volunteered to go out and purchase some cream cakes for the occasion after learning that one of his coworkers was departing. The party was almost finished by the time Rodney arrived with the cakes. Even though he had gone out of his way to contribute, no one had bothered to wait for him. Rodney is offended and humiliated.

You may undoubtedly sympathise with Rodney in these circumstances, but does he really need to take it so personally? Depending on Rodney's past and cognitive style, the occurrence might cause him anything from a major personal insult to a little annoyance. Rodney chooses to use Socratic inquiry to assess his instant response:

1. What exactly are facts?

When I went out to get the cakes, my coworkers did not wait for me to start the morning tea.

2. What are my own perceptions?

They are treating me with contempt. I've been embarrassed. They would have waited for me if they valued me.

3. What proof backs up my beliefs?

They began making morning tea without me.

4. Is there any proof that contradicts my perceptions?

The majority of the personnel is typically pleasant to me. When I arrived with the cakes, several people commented that they should have waited for me.

5. Am I making any logical errors?

I'm rushing to negative assumptions, personalising, and wreaking. This has a bad connotation for me, as it appears to be intentional and personal.

6. In what other way can I interpret this situation?

Most individuals at work are preoccupied with their own problems and do not always consider the needs of others. They didn't wait for me because they forgot — not because they dislike me. People do consider my needs from time to time, but not always. It wasn't anything personal, and it wasn't a huge issue.

BEHAVIOURAL DISPUTING

While utilising logical disputing daily might help us build cognitive flexibility, there are specific instances where it is impossible to use this form of arguing. For example, we may understand that our reasoning is illogical, yet it feels true on a gut level. This is when behavioural disputing might come in handy.

Our actions frequently help to reinforce our current cognitions, even if they are unrealistic or self-defeating. For example, when we treat someone we hate coldly or harshly, we reinforce the notion that they are a horrible person who deserves our contempt. When we postpone addressing a dreadful activity, we reinforce the notion that it is a dreadful duty. When we act arrogantly among our friends, we promote that we are not as good as them. We reinforce the idea that failure is painful when we avoid undertaking tasks that include the risk of failure. By responding in this manner, our cognitions stay unquestioned and are frequently reinforced over time.

While our actions might promote harmful beliefs, they can also be used to refute them. Behaving in ways that contradict particular cognitions might assist us in discovering that certain cognitions are erroneous. Because we question our cognitions with behaviours, this process is known as behavioural disputing. It is also known as behavioural experiments because by changing our behaviour, we provide the chance to learn about the repercussions. The experiment's goal is to determine whether or not our assumptions are right. If the predicted bad results occur, we may employ logical arguing to de-catastrophise, examine the causes for the event, and, if necessary, arrange further behavioural trials using other techniques. If, on the other hand, the bad effects we predicted do not occur, we realise that our impressions were incorrect. Because we learn via experience, behavioural disputing is one of the most potent methods to challenge negative ideas.

Natalie's car was struck from behind twice last year when she was stopped at traffic signals. She experienced serious whiplash on one of those instances. Natalie is now frightened to drive because she feels she will be involved in another accident if she does.

Natalie can logically question her views by actually evaluating the likelihood of another accident and admitting that it is very low. She can also remind herself that she has been driving for over 20 years and has only had a handful of small incidents up until last year.

However, behavioural disputing will be the most strong and effective challenge to Natalie's catastrophic cognitions. Natalie's behavioural assignment will entail getting into her automobile (at first with the help of a supportive buddy) and driving around for small distances. As she learns from experience that there are no bad repercussions, her next step will be to drive alone and progressively expand the distance she travels. She likes to drive on busier routes as her confidence grows. Natalie's catastrophic thinking is directly challenged by the revelation that nothing horrible happens, allowing her to rebuild confidence over time.

Behavioural disputing is a particularly effective technique for facing irrational fears since directly engaging the things we dread enables us to realise on a deeper level that they are not, in fact, harmful.

Goal-Focused Thinking

So far, we've looked at disputing our cognitions logically by explicitly questioning toxic contaminants of our thinking and behaviourally by engaging in behaviours that contradict unrealistic cognitions. Goal-focused thinking is the third point to refute. Recognising the self-defeating character of our cognitions entails thinking about how our present views impede us from attaining our goals. Because we persuade ourselves to release problematic cognitions by admitting their negative consequences, goal-focused thinking is also referred to as "persuasive disputing." It is a motivating approach that encourages us to quit thinking in a self-defeating manner.

When we utilise goal-focused thinking, we remind ourselves to stay focused on the "big picture" – our underlying objectives. As we become aware of the negative repercussions of our current style of thinking, we are driven to change our ways. This is made easier by the following essential question:

- Does thinking or acting in this manner make me feel good or achieve my goals?

When confronted with distressing feelings, we can ask this same question or modify our interrogation to our individual scenario. As an example:

- Does reminding myself that my work must be flawless help me accomplish things on time?
- Is it possible to be happy and have a healthy relationship if I am angry with my partner?
- Is dwelling on the injustice of this circumstance going to help me feel better and go on with my life?
- Does insisting that others share my beliefs make it easier for me to get along with others?
- Is telling myself that I'm a horrible person for making that mistake going to help me have high self-esteem?
- Is stressing about how I look tonight going to help me relax and enjoy the evening?

Goal-focused thinking is beneficial in various situations, but it is especially useful when we are angry, resentful, or frustrated.

Kayla and her husband had travelled to a beach resort with their friends John and Nancy for a vacation. Kayla begins to become irritated by some of John and Nancy's actions after two days. To begin, they are not contributing equally to the purchase of daily provisions. Second, Nancy spends excessive time in the bathroom, and John appears to be even more selfish than Kayla realised. John and Nancy appear to be becoming increasingly irritable as time passes. By day six, even the way they breathe has become irritating!

Kayla's concern is that thinking this way makes her feel awful and ruins her trip. Kayla chooses to employ goal-focused thinking to question her reaction, focusing on the self-defeating character of her cognitions:

'Does thinking this way help me feel good or achieve my goals?' I came here to have fun, but I'm feeling bitter and angry most of the time. I'm simply hurting myself by being upset by their behaviour - I'm spoiling my vacation! I may choose to let go of these sentiments by embracing our differences and not getting caught up in trivial matters.'

Kayla can also use logical reasoning to refute her beliefs:

'They don't give as much as we do, but the sum of money involved is insignificant, and they aren't doing it on purpose. The majority of the things that irritate me are little. They are fundamentally good people, even if they do things differently than we do. It's not that big of a deal.'

13

How To Remove Negativity In Relationships

YOUR KIDS DRIVE YOU INSANE. Your parents are far too dependent on you. Your manager is a jerk. Your partner does not comprehend what you are saying. Your best buddy is never available on call.

How frequently do you become angry, frustrated, or even enraged with the people in your life?

The answer to this issue is critical since interpersonal difficulties are a major source of misery in people's lives. We repeat unpleasant talks in our thoughts and meditate for hours on a perceived insult. Or we get estranged from our friends and loved ones, leaving us feeling lonely, alone, and unwanted.

We construct false mental narratives about other people, attributing to their thoughts and behaviours that may or may not be real but seem cruel and overpowering.

Indeed, you cannot survive with people without encountering an odd misunderstanding. If, on the other hand, you discover that most encounters deplete you emotionally, you should seek methods to strengthen these connections or eliminate certain people from your life.

Consider how you would feel if you had no anxiety about the people in your life. How much clearer would your thoughts be?

How much more energy could you devote to useful, good endeavours?

Although significant individuals in our lives can cause mental discomfort, our connections remain one of the essential aspects of our lives that contribute to long-term pleasure.

14

Can Good Relationships Make You Happy?

THE HARVARD STUDY OF ADULT DEVELOPMENT, formerly known as the Grant Study in Social Adjustments, is one of the longest studies of happiness ever performed. Harvard researchers have been monitoring 268 men who started college in the late 1930s since 1937 to investigate the topic of what makes people happy. They've been with them through war, career, marriage and divorce, parenting and grandparenthood, and old age.

The study's current director, psychiatrist, and Harvard Medical School professor Robert Waldinger, says the long-term data is unequivocal: "Close relationships and social connections keep you happy and healthy." That is the gist of everything. People who were more preoccupied with accomplishment and less interested in connection were less pleased. Humans are fundamentally built for interpersonal relationships."

How can relationships contribute so much to our happiness while simultaneously being a major cause of mental exhaustion? The idea is to cultivate high-quality relationships rather than simply having relationships. A high-quality connection, whether with a love partner, friend, family member, or even a coworker, entails:

- Putting the relationship first.
- Communication that is open and honest.
- Healthy conflict resolution.
- Mutual respect and trust.
- Interests in common.
- Some degree of emotional and/or intellectual closeness.
- Forgiveness and acceptance.
- Physical contact (for personal relationships).

It is in our best interests to be proactive in selecting the people in our lives and engaging with them. Our well-being and peace of mind need to cultivate, maintain, and nurture positive connections. Rather than relying on others to alter your relationships, the greatest place to begin is within yourself. Even if your family, friends, and business partners need to work on their interpersonal skills, you can go a long way toward decreasing stress in your life by making changes in yourself. You can't change others anyhow; all you have control over is how you connect with and respond to the people around you.

Let's look at some strategies to strengthen your connections, which may have a direct and beneficial influence on your attitude.

INCREASE YOUR PRESENCE

Research of "relatively happy, non-distressed couples" conducted by the University of North Carolina discovered that couples who regularly practised mindfulness experienced gains in their marital happiness. They also had lower "relationship stress, stress coping effectiveness, and total stress." Mindfulness practice enables us to be present with our partners, be less emotionally reactive with them, and overcome difficult events in the relationship more quickly.

Relationship presence is not limited to romantic relationships. Mindfulness may be practised in all of your relationships.

What does being more present in your relationships imply?

. . .

EXPERIMENT WITH EMPATHIC LISTENING.

Have you ever observed how certain people do not pay attention during a conversation?

Many people find it difficult to pay attention because their minds are cluttered with so many thoughts. When someone is talking, our minds are often preoccupied with the minutia of our lives, concerns, or what we want to say next.

Empathic (or active) listening is the readiness to go outside of your preoccupied thoughts and listen to their words without judgment. Empathy is the high note of empathic listening because it makes the speaker feel safe, affirmed, and understood.

In the conventional sense, active listening is not part of a discussion. There is no give and take, no sharing of discussion, and no competition to speak. It's all about the other person and what they're trying to communicate—with their words, with the words they don't say, and with their emotions—with empathetic listening.

You must be willing to do the following as an empathic listener:

- Allow the other person to lead the conversation and decide on the topic.
- Maintain full focus on what the other person is saying.
- Even if you have anything essential to say, avoid interrupting.
- Pose open-ended questions that elicit more information from the speaker.
- Avoid jumping to conclusions or giving solutions.
- What you heard the speaker say, reflect back to them.

Although it may appear that empathic listening solely helps the speaker, as the listener, you are in a state of concentrated awareness. It is difficult to be trapped in looping thoughts or be sidetracked by concern or remorse when listening empathically.

Begin practising empathic listening with your partner, family, and close friends. Commit to 10 minutes of active listening in your next conversation when you focus completely on the other person and what they are saying. This will bring you closer to your loved one while also providing a distraction from your busy thoughts.

Mindful Speaking

Negative thinking may cause problems with the quality of your relationships. If you use fearful language, self-condemnation, derogatory statements about others, or self-pity, you only serve to convince people that you are a bad person to be around.

On the other side, by focusing on encouraging good encounters, you may deepen the relationships you already have. For example, Dr John Gottman established via his study that for a relationship to be stable and a marriage to endure, there should be five times as many good interactions between partners as negative interactions. Gottman's results can also be extended to various types of relationships. People are drawn away from conflict and negativity.

The first step toward transformation is always awareness. We urge that you pay great attention to what you say throughout a discussion, especially in your romantic connection. Put a mental filter between your thoughts and words, acknowledging the impact your words may have on one of the most important persons in your life.

Resist the urge to respond to someone's words or behaviour merely. Take a minute to consider your remarks. Even if the other person is irritated or furious, speak in a loving, caring, and polite manner, and attempt to use a calm, non-threatening voice. Those around you will frequently respond in kind when you talk more carefully. Even if they don't, you've given yourself the ability to retain self-control and inner serenity.

Mindful speaking practice improves the quality of your interactions and improves the quality of your inner world.

Meditation on Loving Kindness

The goal of loving-kindness meditation is to cultivate feelings of compassion toward others. You may utilise a loving-kindness meditation to strengthen your connections with certain individuals in your life and eliminate negative thoughts about them. This type of meditation raises our awareness of others as human beings worthy of compassion and love, even when they are tough, reducing interpersonal problems and increasing our well-being. Three studies support this assertion.

First, Stanford University researchers discovered that meditation that focuses on loving-kindness enhances people's emotions of social connectivity.

In addition, according to a University of Utah research, practising loving-kindness meditation "reduced overall levels of perceived hostility, insensitivity, interference, and mockery from others." This unique meditation technique will improve not only your intimate relationships but also your relationship with yourself.

Finally, in a seminal study, researchers discovered that practising loving-kindness meditation for seven weeks enhanced feelings of love, pleasure, happiness, appreciation, pride, optimism, interest, amusement, and awe.

Loving-kindness meditation may be practised anywhere, but start with a brief 10-minute meditation in a peaceful area with no distractions.

Here's a quick way to get into the habit:

- Sit in a comfortable posture, either on the floor with your legs crossed and your hands loosely in your lap or on a chair with your legs uncrossed, feet on the floor, and hands in your lap.
- Close your eyes and take two or three deep cleansing breaths before counting each one from 1 to 10.
- Bring to mind a person to whom you want to convey loving-kindness, and examine their excellent qualities—the light of goodness you see in them—once you are relaxed.
- After a few minutes of focusing on their good traits, mentally repeat the following phrases to your loved one: "May you be happy," "May you be well," and "May you be loved."

There is nothing wrong with slightly changing the language to focus on the needs of the person. There are no unbreakable rules. Instead of saying "you," you might substitute the person's name.

You may also include ideas like:

- May you be safe from both internal and external damage and danger.
- May you be safe and secure.
- May you be free of mental anguish and pain.
- Wishing you a life free of bodily pain and suffering.
- May you have a long and healthy life.
- May you be able to live in this world gladly, quietly, cheerfully, and comfortably.

This meditation practice will improve your relationships and boost your emotional well-being and peace of mind. It is ultimately up to you how you adapt the practice to your circumstances, but it remains at its core a highly transformational process in your efforts toward mental cleansing and peace of mind.

Put an End to Comparing Yourself to Others

"Let us not look at the talents we wish we had or pine away for the gifts that are not ours, but instead do the best we can with what we have." Richardson, B.J.

One of the primary causes of mental conflict and emotional misery is comparing oneself unfavourably to others.

- "Wouldn't it be nice if I were as gorgeous as my friend?"
- "How come I can't be as smart as my brother?"
- "They have a lot more money than us."
- "She travels constantly, and I never get to go anywhere."

These ideas can spin out of control, making us feel awful about ourselves while blaming others for our misery. By comparing ourselves to the accomplishments, assets, or characteristics, we create the scene for the dissolution of potentially satisfying relationships.

Comparison creates so many unpleasant sentiments that it harms more than just your mental health; it also harms your relationships. The more you think about how you compare to others, the worse you feel about yourself and the other person. Envy, jealousy, humiliation, remorse, embarrassment, self-loathing, resentment, and anger are not traits that enhance or make you appealing to others.

"Negative feelings like loneliness, envy, and guilt have a vital role to play in a happy existence; they're bright, blazing indicators that something needs to change," says Gretchen Rubin, author of the New York Times bestselling book The Happiness Project.

We all compare ourselves from time to time, and comparing ourselves may sometimes drive us to develop ourselves or attain something that we see in others. But when comparison leads those "huge, blazing signs" to illuminate, it's time to act.

It takes mental work to detach from comparison and the emotions that accompany it. However, adjusting your reactions to others who have "more" can allow you to forge your path and become the greatest person YOU are intended to be.

Here are three easy and quick activities that might help you stop comparing yourself to others:

Practice 1: Experiment with radical self-acceptance

No amount of comparing, stressing, or ruminating will change who you are, how you look, what you've accomplished, or what you own right now. For the time being, the person you are is all you have.

Instead of rejecting this person, lean into it. Accept it and recognise that you are completely fine right now. Adopting this moment of extreme self-acceptance is freeing and empowering in and of itself.

Practice 2: Change what you can

Reinhold Niebuhr, an American theologian, is well known for his book The Serenity Prayer, in which he states:

God grant me the serenity to accept the things I cannot change
The courage to change the things I can;
And the wisdom to know the difference.

Accepting the calmness, bravery, and wisdom Niebuhr seek will provide you with practical skills to balance your longings and disappointments with realities.

Comparing yourself to those you respect might motivate you to make positive changes, up to your game, and enhance your life. However, no matter how hard you strive, you will never be able to equal a certain person's accomplishments. You may never have the same appearance as your fashion model buddy or become as affluent as your millionaire relative.

Rather than wishing for what you don't have, make decisions based on your inner understanding. What can you do differently? What do you wish to alter? Return to your values and life priorities to help you define your life on your terms, rather than attempting to mimic someone whose beliefs and priorities may differ.

You may still want for what you cannot have, but you must make the best of what you do have. Concentrate on your strengths and keep practising self-acceptance.

Practice 3: Be grateful all of the time

Comparisons blind us to all we already have. We become so focused on what others have and how we don't measure up that we fail to recognise all of the gifts surrounding us. It comes down to choosing to perceive the glass as half full rather than half empty—and expressing gratitude for the water in the glass.

Before you get out of bed in the morning, create a mental note of everything wonderful in your life and dwell on each blessing for a minute or two. Do this before going to bed as well.

Writing in a gratitude diary might help to foster sentiments of appreciation. Mentally go through everything that went well and write it down. Consider what your life would be like without the people you care about, your home, your health, and so on. When you imagine having your blessings taken away, you realise how fortunate you are.

15

Getting Unstuck From The Past

WE DISCUSSED RUMINATING on the past previously in the book and how it may lead to feelings of mental overload. When you reflect on the past, you may discover that many of your thoughts are related to experiences with present people in your life. You relive unpleasant or cruel interactions. You obsess about a failed relationship or a lost love. Perhaps you feel longing and sadness for children who have grown and gone out of the house, friends who have wandered away, or siblings who appear distant.

Perhaps you had relationship trauma that was so deep and devastating that you never really recovered, and it continues to interrupt your life and poison your thinking. Looping these memories might elicit unresolved anger, humiliation, guilt, fear, and sadness.

Because relationships are so important in our lives, it's not unexpected that people from our past might bring us grief weeks, months, or even years after an encounter or relationship has ended. You see these "mind movies" so often that you begin to connect with them. Dragging the past about in this way is a heavy load that drains your vitality and inner serenity.

Sometimes we relive old circumstances in an unconscious

attempt to resolve them, but ruminating simply leaves us trapped in the past and unhappy in the present. How do we break free from our memories of the past so that they do not continue to jail us or link us to people who should no longer be a part of our lives?

Eckhart Tolle, the author of The Power of Now, writes, "We may learn to break the pattern of gathering and to perpetuate old feeling by flapping our metaphorical wings and refraining from consciously focusing on the past, whether it happened yesterday or 30 years ago." Instead of becoming caught up in mental movie-making, we may learn to restore our attention to the pristine, timeless present now rather than keeping circumstances or occurrences alive in our minds."

Isn't it easier said than done?

It is difficult just to dismiss sad memories and force these ideas out of our brains.

It's difficult, but it's not impossible.

And it's well worth the work if you want to free yourself up to have great, loving connections in your current life.

You can't be present with your family and friends today if you're trapped in your thoughts about past relationships and old wounds.

Here are some techniques for clearing the clutter of unpleasant thoughts about the past:

Make the best decisions you can

If there is an unsolved dispute or pain between you and another person, take steps to address the situation. Rather than stewing over the previous incident, begin contact with the other person to work through it, especially if you believe you were "wronged." It is difficult to reach out to someone who has harmed you, but the discomfort of doing so is considerably less than the gradual agony of ruminating on past wrongs.

Anger or hurt can make open dialogue difficult, but learn more about good communication so you can have a fruitful conversation with the other person.

Sharing your thoughts and pain, listening to the other person's point of view, giving or asking for forgiveness, and addressing the relationship's future might all be part of the reconciliation process. Break the "spell" of your internal story about the past by talking about it freely.

A meaningful talk with someone from your past isn't always feasible, but when it is, it might be the best way to break free from the bonds of your memories and pain.

CHALLENGE YOUR STORY

When you mentally repeat an event over and over, your perspective becomes the ultimate reality for you. It appears difficult to see the issue from any other perspective.

You may feel your recollections and perception of the connection are right, while the other person may have a completely different view.

Step into the other person's shoes to test your own understanding. You can accomplish this by answering the following questions:

- How might they perceive what happened between you?
- What could you have done or said that they might have misinterpreted?
- Is it possible that your memories are incorrect?
- Does the other person have a valid point of view?
- Is it conceivable that events did not unfold precisely as you thought they did?

Empathising with the other person alleviates some of the anguish or anger connected with the memory. By questioning your own beliefs and memories, you permit yourself to see the situation in a more positive light.

Make an apology

The person from your past may under no circumstances apologise, but they will always forgive you. You don't have to forgive someone in person, but you may forgive them in your heart and thoughts.

Holding on to your anger and pain prolongs your misery and emotional distress. You forgive to be rid of this pain and to be able to live in the present with a clean mind.

According to best-selling self-improvement author Dr Wayne Dyer, "forgiving people is important for spiritual progress." While it is terrible, your experience with someone who has wounded you is now nothing more than a thought or emotion that you keep with you. These resentment, anger, and hatred thoughts reflect sluggish, debilitating energies that will dis-empower you if you continue to allow them to take space in your mind. You would have greater serenity if you could let them go."

Forgiving someone does not always imply that you are reconciled with them. It implies you let go of resentment and wrath so that it does not poison you further. It might be difficult to forgive, especially if the offender has not accepted responsibility for their actions. But you may start by acknowledging that this individual is doing the best they can with their abilities. When you find yourself dwelling on their previous transgressions, redirect your attention away from them and onto yourself. Recognise your feelings without accusing the other person of them. Ask yourself, "What have I learned as a result of this?" How can I utilise it to better myself?"

As Dr Dyer puts it, "your life is like a play with multiple acts." Some of the characters that enter have small parts to perform, while others have considerably significant ones. Some are bad folks, while others are good. But all of them are required; otherwise, they would not be in the play. Accept them all and go on to the next act."

Offering forgiveness may necessitate forgiving yourself for anything you said or did in a relationship. Reflect frankly on your actions and how they may have harmed or offended the other person. You'll probably come up with a slew of excuses for why you acted the way you did, and you could even have some genuine justifications for your behaviour. However, if any aspect of your behaviour was incorrect, you must admit it and forgive yourself. When you shift your viewpoint on previous mistakes, it becomes easier to forgive yourself. Rather than beating yourself up for past relationship blunders, strive to appreciate the past and consider your acts as a benefit. They were a part of who you were at the time, and you needed to learn from them. You can now go on and forgive yourself, knowing who you want to be and how you want to behave.

16

Mindfulness With Your Partner

THE TWO PREVIOUS methods we mentioned apply to any relationship in your life. However, your love relationship stands out as one that requires special care.

You have the chance for tremendous emotional and personal growth with your spouse or love partner, especially if you regard your partner as someone in your life to teach you something. You can learn to be more current and compassionate as a result of this interaction. However, our love connections provide us with the greatest problems in our lives, producing the most "mental clutter" and distress. Mindfulness in your love relationship provides you with a tool for deepening your connection while lowering stress and tension in your life.

Mindfulness specialist and Emeritus Professor of Medicine Jon Kabat-Zinn defines mindfulness as paying attention to the present moment with a goal while letting go of judgment.

This technique may appear unachievable amid an argument when you just want to strike out at your partner. However, with practice, mindfulness raises our awareness of what we are feeling with our partners and gives us the freedom to choose how we want to act (and respond) with them.

When you can avoid emotional reactions with your spouse or

partner, you feel more focused, peaceful, and capable of resolving difficulties lovingly. This capacity alone can rescue you from days, if not years, of mental and emotional suffering that drains your emotional vitality.

"Mindfulness isn't about suppressing or hiding our emotions," writes psychologist and author Dr Lisa Firestone in an article for Psychology Today. "It's just about establishing a new relationship to our feelings and experiences, one in which we are in control. We can see our thoughts and feelings like a passing train rushing into the station, but we alone decide whether or not to board."

Choosing not to join starts a deliberate connection that fosters healing and closeness rather than discord and hostility. Here are some easy steps you may take to become more present in your marriage or love relationship:

Make the Commitment

With the knowledge that mindfulness will enhance the quality of your relationship with your partner, commit to practising this habit regularly. If you've spent years in an unconscious relationship where you and your spouse are reactive, it will take some effort to retrain yourself to interact differently. However, if you are driven to improve your relationship and minimise stress in your life, you can change.

This is the essential connection in your life, and it influences your mental health and view of everything. Commit to this one technique in your relationship, and you will see an improvement in all aspects of your life.

Put a note in a position where you will see it first thing in the morning to remind you to be present with your spouse when you interact. When you first start this practise, you may need to post reminders throughout the house.

Communicate your Commitment

Your decision to be more aware of your relationship is not

reliant on your partner's shared commitment—but it definitely helps.

Sit down with your spouse when you can talk without interruption and inform him or her of your new strategy. You might say something like, "I've decided I want to be more present and compassionate in my relationship with you." It will bring us closer together and allow us to overcome our disagreements without as much anger or hurt. I've committed to this, and I'd appreciate it if you would do the same."

Your spouse may be perplexed as to what this implies, which leads to the additional activities in this chapter that you might do.

BE EMOTIONALLY present

Being emotionally present in conversation entails being completely tuned in to your discussion partner. If your partner is in discomfort, it means remaining emotionally open to the discomfort and demonstrating empathy.

It also entails paying attention to your partner's body language and reflecting it back, as well as employing eye contact, gentle touch, and nodding to demonstrate that you hear your partner. It usually does not imply making ideas or suggesting methods to "repair" an issue unless your partner specifically requests it. When we strive to do "more" for our partner, we actually inhibit our inherent potential for the emotional present. Attuned presence makes your partner feel less alone in his or her emotions.

This level of emotional resonance with your partner leads to increased intimacy, trust, and security in your relationship.

Listen without being defensive.

When you and your partner are having a conflict or emotionally intense talk, presence means you listen without planning your answer or defence.

Be conscious of your own reactionary emotions, identify them, and acknowledge that they have been aroused, but do not act on them. Return your attention to your partner's remarks and realise that your partner's feelings are as significant as your own.

REFLECT back to your partner

The readiness to reflect on your partner the words you hear from them demonstrates that you are attentively listening. It also shows your partner that you care enough to completely grasp what they are saying to you.

Reflecting entails more than simply repeating what your spouse says. It's a method of verifying that what you heard was really what your partner meant. It initiates a dialogue for clarity and promotes debate about mutual settlement and understanding.

This is an extremely useful mindfulness practice during times of conflict, damaged feelings, or misunderstandings.

COMMUNICATE WITH SINCERITY

Being present with your partner is a mature relationship skill. It implies you can't reply or behave like a kid, employing passive-aggressive words or behaviours like eye-rolling, silent treatment, or sulking. Tantrums and angry outbursts always impede honest, real dialogue. When you have a disagreement with your partner, instead of attacking them or making derogatory remarks, return to the practice of mindfulness. Pay attention to your emotions and wait until you are calm and less defensive before starting a dialogue.

Share your thoughts on the problem without assigning blame or criticism. Explain your perspective on the problem, how it made you feel, and what your partner needs to reestablish your relationship. Listen to your partner's reaction and point of view without becoming defensive.

Look for lessons in conflict

If you pay attention, your love relationship may be a laboratory for personal growth. Conflict is painful and unpleasant, but it gives an excellent chance for learning.

Rather than stewing in your rage after a disagreement, ask yourself these questions:

- Is it conceivable that I'm not entirely correct?

- Is my partner's point of view, to some extent, correct?
- Is this the person I want to be with my partner?
- What have I learned from this conflict?
- What is the underlying issue causing my reactions?
- How are my wounded sentiments impeding my growth?
- How do I want to change as a result of this interaction?

Your responses to these questions will promote healing and self-awareness, allowing you to break free from the inner critic who keeps you frustrated and furious.

Spend uninterrupted time with your partner

Spending quality time with your partner is one of the most beneficial things you can do for the health of your relationship. This is a moment when you are both relaxed and engaged since you are not under the constraints of a job, children, or conflict.

Because life is so hectic and stressful, busy couples frequently have to arrange this time. If this is the case for you, make it a point to schedule a regular date or even 30 minutes of daily quiet time with your spouse where you can talk and reconnect.

The more emotional closeness you share with your partner, the more you protect your relationship from the problems that cause you both pain. Putting in the effort is an investment in your mental clarity and peace of mind.

Let go of certain people

Decluttering your relationships might sometimes involve letting go of those who give you pain. Sometimes the only option is to say goodbye to individuals who continue to harm your mental and emotional well-being.

It's difficult to let go of a relationship, even if it's exhausting, holding you back, blinding you to your actual self, or, worse, toxic or abusive.

We put a lot into our friendships, marriages, business partners, and family members.

Quite frequently, it is one of these personal relationships—a person or individuals with whom we have been closely connected for many years—that causes us the most pain and turmoil. You will reach a moment in one of these relationships when the pain and difficulties exceed the benefits—where the consequences of letting go appear less scary than the misery of staying around.

For example, one of the most difficult things Steve has ever had to do was break off all communication with an ex-girlfriend. After an incredibly difficult yearlong relationship, he felt he couldn't have her in his life, even as a friend. Their interaction was simply too toxic for either of them to find happiness in the presence of the other. So he decided to "force" a permanent separation by flying to Europe and spending eight months without access to a cell phone. While it was difficult, Steve understood that the only way to move on was to create a "cold turkey" environment in which the two of them could not have any type of interaction.

You don't have to leave your country to get out of a terrible relationship, but you might want to consider taking a proactive strategy to remove specific individuals from your life—and make sure you stick to it. Making this last decision isn't simple. However, there are some common elements of disagreement in any relationship that indicate it's time to say goodbye. These are some examples:

- Abuse, whether verbal, emotional, or physical.
- Dishonesty, disloyalty, or deception regularly.
- Core principles that differ or honesty that is questioned.
- Toxicity, negativity, and incompatibility in general.
- Consistent, negative irresponsibility.
- Immaturity and emotional manipulation persist.
- Mental health concerns that are unresolved or untreated.
- Substance Abuse (drugs, alcohol, sex, gambling, pornography).
- Refusal to communicate, resolve issues, or invest in the relationship.

ASIDE FROM THESE more catastrophic issues, a relationship may just run its course. You may discover that, for reasons you don't truly understand, another person detracts from your life rather than enlivens it. You may reach a moment in your life where you simply do not want to cope with the emotional clutter and mess that another person has created in your life. If the person causing your pain is your spouse, a parent or family member, or an adult child, you cannot just end the connection without significant consequences. However, you may better manage these interactions and preserve your mental health by setting firm boundaries and communicating them to the person in question.

Managing or letting go of any relationship takes time. Detaching from someone who has been a big part of your life might take months or years, as well as a lot of sorrow. However, we would be negligent if we did not include this point in your mental decluttering alternatives.

Here are some ideas for getting out of a draining or difficult relationship:

CONSIDER the advantages of not having this person in your life

Giving up on a relationship may feel like giving up or being cruel. If you distance yourself from this individual, you may feel guilty. However, if the connection causes you constant distress, you are not treating yourself with respect.

If you're unsure whether to leave (or keep) the connection, consider how your life would be different if you didn't have this person in it. Do you think you'd be relieved? Liberated? Are you less nervous or stressed?

Consider how your life could improve if you didn't have to deal with the difficulties and worries related to your relationships with this individual. Your judgment may be affected by emotions of guilt or responsibility, but try to assess the benefits of letting go honestly.

CONSIDER the consequences of saying goodbye

When a relationship ends, there are always some repercussions. Your decision will most likely influence others close to you, pushing them to choose sides or at the very least take a stand—which may not be in your favour. As a result, some people may cut you off.

The person you're saying goodbye to may try to undermine you, gossip about you, or injure you in some manner. Their reaction may be more extreme or destructive than you expected, leading things to worsen before they improve. You may discover that the loss of the relationship is more difficult than you anticipated, and you may second-guess yourself.

Before you end a relationship, it's a good idea to consider all of the probable consequences. How do you think each of these events will make you feel? Can you deal with the repercussions, or do you find it more destructive than staying in a toxic relationship?

DEFINE what it means to say "goodbye"

Letting go may indicate the termination of a relationship in which there is no communication or connection. However, this is not always practical or reasonable in all partnerships. Goodbye may also imply abandoning the previous method of connecting to this person in favour of a new, more self-protective approach.

Relationships with family members, adult children, or a previous spouse cannot always be severed completely. However, you may set limits on how much time you spend with these individuals and how you communicate with them to safeguard your mental and emotional health.

Determine what "goodbye" means to you. How much time are you willing to devote to this individual? How and how frequently do you want to connect with them? In your dealings with them, what will you no longer tolerate? Being proactive in making these decisions allows you to feel more in control and relaxed about proceeding.

COMMUNICATE your goals without pointing fingers

Dropping a friend or family member cold turkey with no explanation or dialogue may be the easiest way out—but it isn't the most considerate. Yes, this individual may be draining every last drop of your energy and delight, but they still deserve an explanation, or at the very least a heads-up. You don't have to get into a big, drawn-out argument to say goodbye or reduce your contact. You also don't have to assign blame or cast aspersions. Take the high road and say what you would like to hear if you were in the other shoe.

Person-to-person interactions are typically the ideal method to conduct this topic, but you are the most familiar with this person. If you anticipate drama or anger, a letter or phone call may be preferable to a face-to-face meeting. In any case, try to keep it brief and focused on your own emotions rather than their flaws.

You might remark, "I need a break from our friendship because I feel like we're out of sync, and it's causing me discomfort." I care for you, but I need to take a step back. I didn't want to back down without first saying something."

PREPARE for a bad reaction

No matter how gently you terminate a relationship, the other person (and maybe others with whom you are both involved) will react negatively. It's difficult to predict how someone will behave when they're upset or angry. Try to plan ahead of time for these potential repercussions. This might imply asking a support person to accompany you during expressing your intentions and following the unpleasant talk.

You may need to tell friends and relatives who know the other person about your plans to terminate the relationship. If feasible, try to convey your desire to leave the relationship without disparaging the other person.

Depending on the severity and duration of the relationship you are ending, you may require the assistance of a therapist to help you manage your feelings of loss and pain.

RECOGNISE that it may be a process

For some relationships, letting go is a gradual withdrawal over time. Alternatively, it might be an ending followed by a period of reconciliation, only to be followed by a more permanent ending. Guilt, uncertainty, or loneliness can all cause you to second-guess your decision to let go. It takes returning to the relationship to solidify your resolve to terminate it eventually.

Recognise that letting go of someone dear to you is seldom easy or painless. Allow yourself to proceed slowly if that is the best approach for you.

Allow yourself to grieve

The termination of a relationship that was once close or that you believed might work out eventually is heartbreaking. Yes, you may feel relieved that you are no longer need to cope with the problematic parts of the relationship. You could have greater emotional energy and fewer daily annoyances. On the other hand, grief has a tendency to creeping up on us when we least expect it. Any letting goes process might result in a pocket of sadness that requires time to heal.

Don't attempt to talk yourself out of your sadness or second-guess your choice because your grief is complicated. If you accept sadness as a natural part of the grief process, it will move through you more quickly, allowing you to reclaim the peace of mind and joy lost throughout the relationship.

As you can see, removing people from your life may be difficult, but it can also be beneficial since it allows you to spend more time with the ones who matter.

17

Being Happy

MANY OF OUR decisions and behaviours are motivated by a desire for happiness. Whether we act selfishly or altruistically; work until we are 65 or retire early; enrol in a university degree or drop out of a course; keep the house spotless or neglect housework; take frequent vacations or stay at home; seek a new relationship or end an existing relationship; have children or choose not to have children; join a gym or join the couch potato club, it is the desire to.

Although we all desire to be happy, few of us can describe it precisely. Psychologists have grappled with the word, as have philosophers and sociologists. The most often accepted though the insufficient definition is: a condition of subjective well-being. There is a lot of debate regarding what makes someone happy. According to some experts, happiness is a lasting human feature − a persistent belief that life is good, important, and enjoyable. Others say that it is a fleeting condition, that humans have moments of happiness rather than a continuing sense of contentment. Regardless of how we define happiness, it appears that some people are more inclined than others to feel happy with their life.

Since the 1960s, studies on the topic of happiness have been published in peer-reviewed journals. Many have attempted to quantify people's happiness and discover the elements that influence whether or not they are happy. In the late 1980s, two American social psychologists, David Myers and Ed Diener examined the findings of sixteen worldwide research involving 170,000 participants from sixteen different nations. They studied people's happiness ratings in nations worldwide to see what factors predicted whether or not they were happy. One of their unexpected findings was that the variables that predict happiness are remarkably consistent across countries and cultures. Here's what they discovered.

Factors Associated With Happiness

WEALTH: There is much evidence to support the ancient adage, 'Money does not buy happiness.' People with higher earnings are less happy than those with lower incomes. The exception is those who live in poverty, who are far less happy than other people. Poor people, for example, are significantly less pleased than those who are better off in the poorest nations, such as India and Bangladesh. However, it appears that as long as people have enough money to acquire the necessities of life, they may be happy, and having a lot more does not make them happy.

Age and gender do not influence people's happiness levels. Every age group, and both men and women, have an equal amount of happy and sad people. People's race and education level are also unrelated to their degree of happiness.

WORK: This may have a significant impact on people's happiness. Those who feel mission, identity, purpose, or connection with others are more likely to be happy.

Consumption interests can also contribute to happiness. Having a love for anything we do (for example, golf, gardening, music, writing, tennis, bridge, bowls, or dance) and engaging in it regularly enhance our chances of feeling happy.

. . .

GOALS: These can also contribute to people's overall happiness. Having a sense of goal, purpose, or working towards something essential contributes to our happiness.

RELATIONSHIPS: The quality of our relationships is one of the most powerful determinants of happiness. Higher levels of happiness are connected with close, committed, and lasting relationships. People who have personal relationships are more likely to be content than those with many surface interactions but little closeness. Being happily married is also a major predictor of total happiness, yet single individuals are happier than unhappily married.

RELIGION: People deeply spiritually dedicated are more likely to be happy than those who are not. This might be because religious beliefs provide people with a sense of connection and purpose, making their lives more meaningful. People who have strong religious convictions usually have good social support through 'communal fellowship,' which may explain why they are more likely to be happy.

ACTIVE LIFESTYLE: Happy people live active, vigorous lives and are less self-centred than sad ones.

18

Happy People's Attributes

Aside from lifestyle variables, the researchers discovered that four important human characteristics were linked to higher happiness levels.

Good self-esteem: People with high self-esteem are more likely to be happy than those with low self-esteem.

Sense of control: People who believe they have control over their lives are more likely to be happy.

Optimism: People who are upbeat about the future are more likely to be happy.

Extroversion: People who are extroverted and readily associate with others are more likely to report feeling happy.

. . .

ACCORDING to the findings of these and other studies, human happiness is partly influenced by our personal qualities (such as self-esteem, sense of control, optimism, and extroversion) and in part by how we conduct our lives (our work, interests, goals, and interpersonal relationships).

Much of the focus of this book has been on our thoughts – getting to know ourselves better, recognising the cognitions that make us unpleasant (i.e., angry, sad, worried, depressed, frustrated, or worthless), and working actively to change those cognitions. Using the cognitive and behavioural methods discussed in this book might help us feel better in situations when we would otherwise feel bad. It can also help us acquire more characteristics linked with human pleasure, such as a sense of control over our experiences, positive self-esteem, optimism, and a higher willingness to take social risks and interact with others.

LIFESTYLE

How we spend our time from day to day, week to week, and month to month can significantly influence how we feel. Our way of life impacts whether we are happy or unhappy, anxious or relaxed, lonely or connected, healthy or ill, bored or stimulated, contented or unfulfilled. The way we spend our time frequently reflects our ideas about what is essential to us. For example, if you spend a lot of time on job-related activities, it's usually because you value employment and the benefits it provides. If you spend a lot of time on leisure activities, chances are you feel that having fun is essential; if you spend a lot of time studying, chances are you believe that education and the benefits it will provide are worthwhile.

However, our views may not always correspond to how we live our lives. For example, you may feel that your health is essential but spend relatively little time exercising or other good lifestyle practices. Or you may believe in the importance of relationships yet make little effort to maintain friendships or spend time with people you enjoy. Alternatively, you may feel that leisure is essential but spend very little time doing things you love.

While there is no right or wrong way to spend our time, it may be beneficial to reflect on our present way of life and ask ourselves if it is compatible with our values and aspirations. After this section, the lifestyle self-assessment questionnaire might assist us in reviewing various elements of our lifestyle and identifying areas that may benefit from the change.

QUESTION YOURSELF:

- How happy are you with your current way of life?
- Does it represent your beliefs about what is important to you?
- Is it beneficial to one's happiness and health?
- Will your current way of life provide you with the things you desire in the future?

A BALANCED LIFESTYLE enhances the chances of feeling happy for the majority of people. This entails focusing our time and energy on various activities rather than placing all of our eggs in one basket. People who have leaned too much on one aspect of their life will attest that if we drop our basket (due to retrenchment, divorce, health difficulties, or financial troubles), we may get ourselves into a lot of difficulties. Spending energy on a variety of activities is not only a safer bet for the future, but it also enriches and fulfils our lives in the present.

While there are many various sorts of activities that people like, a healthy balance entails devoting some time and effort to each of the following areas:

- Work/regular responsibilities.
- Hobbies/recreational activities.
- Mental exercise.
- Maintenance of health.
- Relationships.
- Work/regular obligations.

Do you like how you spend your time during the week, whether at work or doing other things?

When most individuals are engaged in some regular labour or activity, they feel happy. Although there is no reason why it should take up five days a week or fall within specific hours, a commitment to regular action — whether paid job, volunteer work, education, or a hobby — may have several benefits. Regular commitments organise our week and give us a purpose to get out of bed in the morning. Even though we instinctively want to sleep in, the discipline that comes with regularity appears to make the majority of us feel and operate better.

Other benefits of work or a regular activity include cerebral stimulation, social interaction, enjoyment, purpose, a sense of success, self-efficacy, personal fulfilment, and high self-esteem. It also lowers our chances of being depressed. One of the main determinants of total life happiness is rewarding employment.

On the other hand, work may be boring, frustrating, and soul-destroying, and for some individuals, leaving or retiring is the greatest life-enhancing move they can make. One of the paradoxes of work is that it may be our greatest source of happiness and fulfilment, or it can be our biggest cause of unhappiness, stress, isolation, and health problems.

We are more likely to experience dissatisfaction and despair if we have too much time on our hands or too few hobbies. Many of the benefits that come with meaningful employment (such as routine, social interaction, stimulation, a sense of purpose, and so on) may be experienced by those who are not in paid work by participating in activities such as volunteer work, education, or regular hobbies.

INTERESTS/RECREATIONAL activities

What kinds of things do you do for fun and relaxation? Do you get enough enjoyment out of life?

Leisure activities include anything we do for fun and pleasure. Different people have different interests. Sports, crafts, bushwalking, sailing, movies, eating out, social media, artwork, bridge, playing a musical instrument, computer gaming, and dancing are all popular pastimes. Leisure activities give enjoyment and relaxation while also providing a break from one's daily routine. They also provide a counterweight to the pressures and strains of our daily life. One of the advantages of not working is that we have more time to engage in recreational activities.

Watching television is the most common type of leisure activity in modern Western countries such as ours. Some individuals are extremely critical of television because of the low quality of many shows and the many commercials on commercial television channels. Watching television is also a passive activity; it diverts our attention from other activities and inhibits social contact or participation in more creative or challenging activities. This is especially problematic for youngsters, who frequently watch television for many hours each day. While television may be a fantastic source of entertainment, education, relaxation, and cerebral stimulation, it can also negatively impact our lives when used excessively or inappropriately. Excessive TV viewing deprives us of other, more valuable activities – we might be reading, talking to others, solving a problem, walking, discussing, entertaining, playing sports, or any of a plethora of other activities. In addition, watching indiscriminately exposes us to meaningless trash and inane advertisements – why subject ourselves to this when there are so many other, more helpful things we might be doing?

Some people feel guilty when they indulge in recreational activities because they believe they should always be "productive" with their time. This comes from inflexible ideas, typically taught as a kid, that enjoyable activities are somehow less genuine than those that require hard labour and generate visible results. However, if we do not engage in leisure activities in a spirit of guilt-free pleasure, we will not fully appreciate the experience. Is there any purpose in taking part only half-heartedly?

Mental stimulation

What types of activities do you engage in for mental stimulation?

Our brain thrives on stimulus. Acquiring new knowledge, thinking critically, questioning our own beliefs, and solving issues are among the most gratifying activities for most people because they train our minds. Reading, writing, studying, doing puzzles, working, watching excellent quality TV shows, listening to the radio, playing games, seeing films, going to the theatre, and having dialogues with other people are all activities that may exercise our minds. Indeed, many of us like nothing more than a good argument with friends over dinner.

Mentally stimulating activities are pleasurable in and of themselves, and they enrich our lives. Exercising the brain also aids in the maintenance of healthy mental function in old age. The ancient adage, "Use it or lose it," applies to the brain as well as other areas of the body. Furthermore, activities that stimulate the 'right side of the brain' - those that move us on a spiritual level,' such as music, art, poetry, dance, theatre, meditation, or any creative passion — enable us to maintain a healthy balance between the intellectual and creative sides of our minds.

Health maintenance

How much responsibility do you accept for your health?

Physical health was commonly thought to be a matter of luck among previous generations – if you were lucky, you had good health; if you weren't, you fell ill or died young. Medical research has proven the link between behaviour and health throughout time. We have grown to appreciate the value of good lifestyle choices such as not smoking, regular exercise, a balanced diet, enough sleep, and avoiding excessive quantities of alcohol or drugs. Stress management and supportive social interactions have lately been added to the list of good lifestyle practices. Although the 'genetic lottery' that determines one's predispositions still has an element of chance, our lifestyle choices may significantly impact how well we feel and how long we live. Given that most of us already know what we need to do to improve our odds of remaining healthy, it's surprising that so many of us don't do it.

The ability to exert self-control in connection to healthy living practices is partially determined by one's ability to withstand frustration. Low frustration tolerance might hinder our motivation to attain our goals because we prioritise instant satisfaction above long-term interests. Motivating ourselves to stop self-defeating behaviours such as smoking, overeating, excessive drinking, drug abuse, or lack of exercise necessitates making our health a high priority. Furthermore, we must establish clear objectives, devise a plan of action, and be prepared to deal with the inevitable roadblocks that will occur along the way.

Relationships

How much time do you spend with the people you care about? Are relationships important to you?

Humans are social animals. We love conversing with and being with people because it is in our nature – we are naturally built to connect. Although we might be quite content spending time alone, we instinctively want to be among others.

The quality of our social interactions strongly influences our total happiness. As a result, activities that strengthen our bonds with people tend to boost our happiness. Good connections offer us several emotional and practical rewards. They meet our desire for social connection and belonging, make us feel safe, and contribute to our sense of self-worth. They also give entertainment, amusement, and cerebral stimulation. When we are attempting to solve issues, other people can provide us with ideas, helpful information, a new viewpoint, and, in some cases, practical aid. Several studies have discovered that good supporting relationships are helpful not just to our psychological well-being but also to our physical health.

Men's social behaviour differs from that of women in some intriguing ways. Besides their partner and close family, males in most households bear minimal responsibility for maintaining social ties. Women are more often in charge of establishing social plans and are more likely to contact friends. They are also more likely than males to develop intimate connections with persons who are not members of their family unit, generally other women. Although strong social support is equally vital for men and women, men are less likely to initiate contact or sustain social relationships and rely more on their partner for companionship, closeness, and social support. As a result, males frequently have fewer tools to assist them in dealing through times of marriage breakup or loss. Losing a spouse typically has a more severe impact on men's health than on women's, owing to the more restricted support available to males.

While having a loving and supportive primary connection is fantastic, relying on one person to provide all of our emotional needs is hazardous, similar to placing all of our eggs in one basket. Developing at least a few close friendships, rather than relying on one person to satisfy all of our social and emotional requirements, is a safer and psychologically better strategy.

Time and communication are two key components for maintaining good partnerships. Maintaining helpful connections necessitates making ourselves available – spending time with others and, at times, initiating contact. This may be challenging for people who have a busy life. Friendships might suffer due to the pressures of hard work, family duties, or a new love interest. If we are fortunate, we will recognise the mistake of our ways in time to correct it; if not, loneliness, isolation, or despair will ultimately drive home the cost of neglecting our relationships. Sharing a regular activity, such as going to the movies, concerts, meals, athletic events, going on walks, or participating in sports, can give a structure for staying in touch.

Open communication is the second essential component for healthy partnerships. Self-disclosure – communicating openly about our experiences, ideas, and feelings — is what binds us to others. Communication continuously courteous, professional, or 'edited' creates a barrier between individuals, regardless of how much we wish to connect. Self-disclosure and open communication are essential components of healthy partnerships. Of course, this does not imply that every conversation should be filled with in-depth and profound disclosures of our deepest emotions. However, it does imply that we are willing to speak frankly and share our emotions at times. Balance is essential in communication, as it is in everything else.

Living with Purpose – Set Life Goals

We've previously seen how creating and working toward objectives may help us overcome depression and build resilience in the long run. Setting goals may also assist us in problem-solving and gaining control over some of life's obstacles. Finally, creating goals can inspire us to make positive changes in our lives.

Many of the essential things to us may be accomplished by identifying what we want, developing a plan of action, and following through on it. Defining life goals allows us to focus on what we want and inspires us to mobilise our resources to achieve them.

Afterword

Mind training is the mental counterpart of housekeeping. It's a daily ritual that must be followed to keep on track. However, training your mind is not as basic or straightforward as housework. Managing your ideas requires dedication and effort. It also necessitates regular, if not moment-to-moment, awareness of your mental state and the antics of your monkey mind.

If left to its own devices, your mind will swing from branch to branch, pursuing a distraction or stewing in the sour juice of hatred or anger. It may also linger in daydreaming and imagination, which are considerably more pleasant but uncontrolled states of mind. When you fail to take stock of your mental clutter, your thoughts and emotions become erratic and unpredictable. As a result, your daily experience becomes unpredictable and completely dependent on the randomness of thinking.

The intrusive ideas you have throughout the day highlight the perplexing fact that many of the mind processes appear to be beyond conscious control. To make matters worse, our thoughts are quite real and strong, and they have a significant influence on our views of the world. Allow yourself to forget for a minute that your random ideas have any value. What if those troublesome ideas aren't any more true or substantial than random graffiti on a wall?

There may be some link to a memory or feeling, but they do not represent reality in the present time. This is, for the most part, the reality about thinking.

Although your subconscious mind will never give you total control over your thoughts, you can control some of them. You may also modify your behaviours and routines to handle them better and the feelings they elicit.

Throughout this book, we have provided a wide range of ideas and techniques for organising your mind so that you may silence the negative voice in your head, feel less stress, and enjoy more peace of mind. Getting rid of negativity in your thoughts is a lifetime process, but it pays off with deep rewards that may greatly influence your quality of life. The less time you spend "in your mind" with distracting, unpleasant ideas, the more time you will have to appreciate the present moment—and every present moment for the rest of your life.

You know what it takes to feel less concerned about all the "stuff" that goes on in your brain. We now implore you to act. Begin today with the most difficult problem in your life and commit to resolving it within the next week.

Feedback

Thank you for reading 'How To Remove Negative Thinking From Your Life'. We hope you enjoyed the book? Please now scan the QR code below to leave your feedback.

Feedback

Thank you for reading "How To Reduce Stress for Happier Daily Life". We hope you enjoyed the book. Please scan the below QR code below to leave your feedback.

Claim Your Freebie NOW!

Get Good At Problem Solving

Want to know the secret behind getting good at problem solving? Everyone seems to be able to do it, but you're stuck in the pile of endless to-do lists with little progress.

Ok, so how do I get my FREE book?

EASY! See the next page

Claim Your Freebie NOW

Instructions:

1. Open the camera or the QR reader application on your smartphone.
2. Point your camera at the QR code to scan the QR code.
3. A notification will pop-up on screen.
4. Click on the notification to open the website link

Claim Your Free NOW

Instructions:

1. Open the camera of the QR code application on your smartphone.
2. Point the camera at the QR code to scan the QR code.
3. Identification: Tap to open the page.
4. Open or the notification to open the web structure.

SCAN ME

Also By Rachel Stone

Start Being Fearless, Stop Being Scared

Fed up of being scared of the things in life that hold you back? It's time to take control back and start being fearless.

Also By Rachel Stone

Why Living a Simple Life is Better for You

An easy guide to help you change the way you think about your life. Take steps to start living a stress-free life.

Also By Rachel Stone

How To Heal Toxic Thoughts

Are you sick of your whole day being ruined due to your overthinking? Have you had enough of self-sabotaging everything good in your life? Do you want practical strategies to finally have a peaceful night's sleep?

Grab the Rachel Stone series NOW

Instructions:

1. Open the camera or the QR reader application on your smartphone.
2. Point your camera at the QR code to scan the QR code.
3. A notification will pop-up on screen.
4. Click on the notification to open the website link

Grab the Kindred and Stone series NOW

Instructions:

1. Open the camera or the QR reader app in your Smartphone.
2. Hold your camera steady. QR code must scan like a QR scanner app/audio app and a pop-up for screen.
3. Click on the notification to open the website link.

www.ingramcontent.com/pod-product-compliance
Lightning Source LLC
Chambersburg PA
CBHW031545080526
44588CB00018B/2707